PATHWAYS

ACTIVITIES *for*

INTEGRATED SOFTWARE

Minta Berry

SettingPace
Cincinnati, Ohio

JOIN US ON THE INTERNET
WWW: http://www.thomson.com
EMAIL: findit@kiosk.thomson.com   A service of I(T)P®

South-Western Educational Publishing
an International Thomson Publishing company I(T)P®

Cincinnati • Albany, NY • Belmont, CA • Bonn • Boston • Detroit • Johannesburg • London • Madrid
Melbourne • Mexico City • New York • Paris • Singapore • Tokyo • Toronto • Washington

Managing Editor: Carol Volz
Project Manager: Dave Lafferty
Marketing Manager: John Wills
Design Coordinator: Mike Broussard
Development & Production Services: SETTINGPACE
Writing: Mary Colleen McLaughlin

ISBN: 0-538-72033-6

3 4 5 6 PN 02 01 00 99

Printed in the United States of America

I⟨T⟩P ®

International Thomson Publishing

South-Western Educational Publishing is a division of International Thomson Publishing, Inc. The ITP logo is a registered trademark used herein under license by South-Western Educational Publishing.

The names of all commercially available software and other products mentioned herein are used for identification purposes only and may be either trademarks, registered trademarks, and/or copyrights of their respective owners. South-Western Educational Publishing disclaims any affiliations, associations, or connection with, or sponsorship or endorsement by such owners.

TABLE OF CONTENTS

Word Processing Activities

Spreadsheet Activities

Database Activities

Integrated Activities

ACTIVITY 1   Creating and Saving a Document

OBJECTIVES   **Estimated Time: 20 minutes**

- Create a new document
- Use word wrap feature
- Save a document

You have just read an advertisement for a one-day seminar on how to be an effective communicator. The workshop sounds like something you would like to attend. Write the following short memo to your manager requesting time to attend this workshop.

INSTRUCTIONS

1. Create a new document.

2. Key the document below.

3. Use word wrap and press the ENTER key twice between paragraphs.

4. Save the document as ACT001.

5. Close the document.

Current Date

Maureen Margolies, Department Manager

EFFECTIVE COMMUNICATION SKILLS WORKSHOP

At our last performance evaluation meeting, we discussed possible workshops that would help me to be a more effective communicator.

I have good news, Raymond Walters College is offering a one-day workshop on effective communication skills. The workshop will present communication skills in the following areas: giving effective presentations; handling people in difficult situations; leading and conducting meetings; using effective telephone skills; and providing effective customer service.

This workshop is offering the necessary skills that I could use in my position. With your permission, I would like to attend this workshop. The workshop is scheduled for June 5, 9:00 a.m. to 4:30 p.m., at Raymond Walters College, in Blue Ash.

Please let me know so that I can send in my reservation form. If you would like to see the advertisement, please call me.

Your Full Name

ACTIVITY 2   Creating and Saving a Document

OBJECTIVES

Estimated Time: 20 minutes

- Create a new document
- Use word wrap feature
- Save a document

Your manager has asked you to key the following letter.

INSTRUCTIONS

1. Create a new document.
2. Key the document on the next page.
3. Use word wrap and press the ENTER key twice between paragraphs.
4. Save the document as ACT002.
5. Close the document.

Current Date

Mr. Taylor Markham, President
Human Resources Manager
Powers, Inc.
189 Central Avenue
Chicago, IL 54012

Dear Mr. Markham

I was pleased to receive your letter requesting enrollment in the Seventh Annual Leadership conference being held April 18 and 19 at the Mariner Inn in San Francisco.

As a manager, you obviously recognized the need to be an effective manager as well as a leader who inspires and serves as a role model for all employees of Powers, Inc. This week-long conference will introduce you to the latest trends in human resource management and leadership training. Strategies will be introduced through small-group workshops to assist you in enabling growth, teamwork, innovation, and risk taking.

An additional highlight of the week will be the keynote speaker on Friday morning. This year we are pleased to announce that Dr. Janice Logan will share her vast experience in the area of leadership training. I look forward to sharing this conference with you. Your enrollment is complete and you should receive an enrollment package soon.

Sincerely

Rebecca S. Watson
Conference Director

ACTIVITY 3

Inserting Text

OBJECTIVES

Estimated Time: 25 minutes

• Scroll through text with mouse or cursor control keys
• Insert punctuation
• Insert words

   You're in a hurry to send the following memo to your department chair before she leaves for a meeting. After typing the memo, you realize that you left out commas, characters, and words.

INSTRUCTIONS

1. Create a new document.
2. Key the following memo as displayed.

Current Date

R Corgan, Department Chair

OA FACULTY WORKSHOP

Wayne Brachman President of Creative Presentations has agreed to be the speaker for our faculty workshop.

Wayne has given over hundred presentations and talks to several organizations such as Procter and Wilson, Central Public Schools, American Youth Association, Eye Shades, etc.He has provided the enclosed brochure and letters of references.

I have called three of the references and they have given Wayne outstanding recommendations. Based on this information, the committee is recommending Wayne Brachman as our speaker for our OA workshop.

Rose White

---

3. Save the document as ACT003.
4. After keying the memo, make the changes shown on the next page to this memo.

Current Date

R Corgan, Department Chair
Office Administration
(OA) FACULTY WORKSHOP

Wayne Brachman, President of Creative Presentations, has agreed to be the speaker for our faculty workshop.

Wayne has given over hundred presentations and talks to several organizations such as Procter and Wilson, Central Public Schools, American Youth Association, Eye Shades, etc. He has provided the enclosed brochure and letters of references.

I have called three of the references and they have given Wayne outstanding recommendations. Based on this information, the committee is recommending Wayne Brachman as our speaker for our OA workshop.

M.
Rose White

5. Proofread the document and make other corrections as needed.

6. Save the revised document.

7. Close the document.

ACTIVITY 4 Inserting Text

OBJECTIVES **Estimated Time: 25 minutes**

- Scroll through text with mouse or cursor control keys
- Split one paragraph into two paragraphs
- Insert hard returns

At a recent business luncheon, you sat across from a human resource manager of a local bank. He was interested in the internship program your college offers. As a follow up to this conversation, you want to send this manager information about your program.

INSTRUCTIONS

1. Create a new document.

2. Key the following letter as displayed.

Mr. Christian Logan
Human Resource Manager
Taylor National Bank
301 Vine Street
Cincinnati, OH 45202

Dear Mr. Logan

Here is the internship program information you requested. As I mentioned to you at the Rotary Club luncheon, the internship program is designed for students to begin at the end of their freshman year. Students must complete requirements before being accepted into this program. They must have completed at least 45 credit hours of Freshman English, computer literacy, word processing, and typing before entering the program. Also, students must have a minimum grade point average of 3.0.

Once they are accepted into the program, most students work full time during the summer and approximately 20 hours per week during the sophomore year. Students take classes in the mornings and work at their internship positions in the afternoons or on Tuesdays and Thursdays.

The program provides excellent opportunities for both the employer and student. Employers are happy with the quality of student they have in the intern position; and employers are willing to help students gain valuable work experience. They bring that experience into the classroom to complement the textbook theory.

Please call Vicki Hammer, our internship coordinator. She will be glad to discuss the program in more detail. She can be reached at 555-1212.

Sincerely
Rose M. Corgan

Enclosures

3. Save the document as ACT004.

4. Make the following changes to this letter.

Mr. Christian Logan *← current date with 4 hard returns*
Human Resource Manager
Taylor National Bank
301 Vine Street
Cincinnati, OH 45202

Dear Mr. Logan *(:)*

Here is the internship program information you requested. As I mentioned to you at the Rotary Club luncheon, the internship program is designed for students to begin at the end of their freshman year. Students must complete requirements before being accepted into this program. They must have completed at least 45 credit hours of Freshman English, computer literacy, word processing, and typing before entering the program. Also, students must have a minimum grade point average of 3.0.

Once they are accepted into the program, most students work full time during the summer and approximately 20 hours per week during the sophomore year. Students take classes in the mornings and work at their internship positions in the afternoons or on Tuesdays and Thursdays.

The program provides excellent opportunities for both the employer and student. Employers are happy with the quality of student they have in the intern position; and employers are willing to help students gain valuable work experience. They bring that experience into the classroom to complement the textbook theory.

Please call Vicki Hammer, our internship coordinator. She will be glad to discuss the program in more detail. She can be reached at 555-1212.

Sincerely, *← insert 3 hard returns after closing*
Rose M. Corgan
asst. Professor
Enclosures

---

5. Proofread the revised document and make other corrections as needed.

6. Save the revised document.

7. Close the document.

ACTIVITY 5 — Deleting Text

OBJECTIVES

Estimated Time: 30 minutes

- Delete text using the **DELETE** key
- Delete text using the **BACKSPACE** key

You are an administrative assistant in the human resources department of a small manufacturing plant. Your boss asks you to write a memo to the plant employees reminding them they are not following suggested safety precautions while working. You are to remind them of safety procedures.

INSTRUCTIONS

1. Create a new document.

2. Key the following memo as displayed.

TO: All Employees

FROM: Alice C. Wheeler

DATE: May 25, 1996

SUBJECT: Plant Safety Requirements

Every year the Human Resources department likes to remind employees of safety requirements for the office and plant area. This reminder seems to be necessary since time seems to have a way of making us a little less vigilant regarding safety measures. For your safety and those of visitors we would like to remind your of the importance of following all these requirements. Compliance of the following rules while in the plants area must be followed:

Hard hats and eye protection goggles must be worn at all times.

Heeled shoes over 2 inches and open-toed sandals are restricted from the area.

Long hair must be tied back so as not to become entangled in machinery.

Scarves and ties are not permitted.

Your safety while working at Hillcrest Manufacturing is a priority concern of management. Thank you for cooperating with these important regulations.

---

3. Save the document as ACT005.

You have decided that a memo is too impersonal and due to the seriousness of the contents regarding safety procedures, a personal letter would be better.

4. Edit the memo, deleting and inserting text as instructed. Delete text to the left of the insertion point by striking the **BACKSPACE** key. Delete the text to the right of the insertion point by striking the **DELETE** key.

5. Use the selection procedure to highlight blocks of text such as sentences or paragraphs.

TO: All Employees

FROM: ~~Alice C. Wheeler~~

DATE: ~~May 25, 1996~~

SUBJECT: Plant Safety Requirements

delete

Insert: current date
Inside address: Mr. Jon Arthur
1293 Rainbow Terrace
Mt. Lookout, OH 45032
Salutation: Dear Jon

Every year the Human Resources department likes to remind employees of safety requirements for the office and plant area. This reminder ~~seems to be~~ *is* necessary since time seems to have a way of making us ~~a little~~ less vigilant regarding safety measures. For your safety and those of visitors, we would like to remind you of the importance of following all these ~~requirements~~ *regulations*. Compliance of the following rules while in the plant area must be followed:

Hard hats and eye protection goggles must be worn at all times.

Heeled shoes over *two* 2 inches and open-toed sandals are restricted from the area.

Long hair must be tied back so as not to become entangled in machinery.

Scarves and ties are not permitted.

Your safety while working at Hillcrest Manufacturing is a ~~priority~~ concern of management. Thank you for cooperating with these important regulations.

Sincerely yours,

Madeline Cole, Director
Human Resources Department

---

6. Save the revised document.

7. Close the document.

ACTIVITY 6   Deleting Text

OBJECTIVES   **Estimated Time: 20 minutes**

- Select text by using the menu options, keyboard commands, or shortcut commands
- Delete text by selecting and pressing the **DELETE** key

You have been invited to speak at a community women's club. Due to previous commitments you are unable to speak, and you write a letter declining the invitation. You compose your first draft at the computer.

INSTRUCTIONS

1. Create a new document.

2. Key the following document as displayed.

Current Date

Ms. Anne Mason
Westchester Women's Club
1000 Manchester Road
Westchester, KY 46091

Dear Mrs. Mason:

I'm sorry that I will not be able to speak to your Women's group on the topic of dealing with difficult people. The topic is one that I truly enjoy giving.

Thank you for the kind words about recommendations you've received about my "difficult people" speech. I guess that's because I've dealt with so many difficult people!

The Westchester's Women's Club is a wonderful philanthropic organization, and I would be honored to speak to your group. However, due to a long-standing personal committment on that date, it will be necessary for me decline at this time.

If you are in need of a speaker at a future WWC meeting, please call me as soon as you know. I look forward to presenting to your group in the future.

Sincerely,

Alice Horton, CEO
Days Incorporated

---

3. Save the document as ACT006.

After reviewing your letter for final edit, you detect a negative tone and decide that by deleting some of the negative wording you would project a more positive image.

4. Use the select and delete method to delete blocks of text. Make all changes as indicated.

Current Date

Ms. Anne Mason
Westchester Women's Club
1000 Manchester Road
Westchester, KY 46091

Dear Mrs. Mason:

I'm sorry that I will not be able to speak to your Women's group on the topic of dealing with difficult people. The topic is one that I truly enjoy giving.

Thank you for the kind words about recommendations you've received about my "difficult people" speech. I guess that's because I've dealt with so many difficult people!

The Westchester's Women's Club is a wonderful philanthropic organization, and I would be honored to speak to your group. However, due to a long-standing personal commitment on that date, it will be necessary for me to decline at this time.

If you are in need of a speaker at a future WWC meeting, please call me as soon as you know. I look forward to presenting to your group in the future.

Sincerely,

Alice Horton, CEO
Days Incorporated

---

5. Save the revised document.

6. Close the document.

ACTIVITY 7   Using Open and Save As

Requires ACT001 from Activity 1

OBJECTIVES

Estimated Time: 15 minutes

- Open an existing document
- Save a document with a different name

    You have just read an advertisement for a one-day seminar you would like to attend. Make appropriate changes to a memo you have used previously to request time off to attend a workshop.

INSTRUCTIONS

1. Open the document ACT001.
2. Make the changes indicated below.
3. Use save as to save the document with a new filename—ACT007.
4. Compare the documents ACT001 and ACT007
5. Close both documents.

Date of memo: January 11, 1997

Date of workshop: February 26, 1997

ACTIVITY 8

Using Open and Save As

Requires ACT002 from Activity 2

Estimated Time: 15 minutes

OBJECTIVES

- Open an existing document
- Save a document with a different name

Your manager has asked you to send the same letter to a second person.

INSTRUCTIONS

1. Open the document ACT002.
2. Make the changes indicated below.
3. Use save as to save the document with a new filename—ACT008.
4. Compare the documents ACT002 and ACT008
5. Close both documents.

Inside address:	Morgan P. Tamulavitch MPT Enterprises 760 Anthony Plaza St. Louis, Missouri 63111
Salutation:	Dear Ms. Tamulavitch
Company name in body of letter:	MPT Enterprises

ACTIVITY 9   Adding Headers and Footers

OBJECTIVES   **Estimated Time: 20 minutes**

- Create a new document
- Add a header
- Add a footer

You have been asked to prepare a some basic instructions about using headers and footers.

INSTRUCTIONS

1. Create a new document.

2. Key the document shown below.

3. Save the document as ACT009.

4. Add a header that reads: This is a header.

5. Add a footer that reads: This is a footer.

6. Save and close the document.

Headers and footers are text blocks that appear at the top and bottom of a page. Text that appears at the top of a page is called a header; text that appears at the bottom of a page is called a footer.

How you add headers and footers to documents depends on the word processing software that you are using.

If you are using Microsoft Works, you can follow the steps outlined below to create headers and footers.

1. Select View from the main menu.
2. Next, select Headers and Footers.
3. Create a simple, one-line header by keying the text in the header box.
4. Use the tab key or mouse to move to the footer box; key the text for a one-line footer.
5. Press the Enter key or click on the OK box.

ACTIVITY 10   Adding Headers and Footers

OBJECTIVES   **Estimated Time: 20 minutes**

+ Create a new document
+ Add a header
+ Add a footer

You have been asked to create a list of holidays that will be observed at your company. Key the following list of holidays. Add a header to the page to indicate that the list should be posted on department bulletin boards. Add a footer to identify the name of the document.

INSTRUCTIONS

1. Create a new document.
2. Key the document shown below.
3. Save the document as ACT010.
4. Add the header shown below.
5. Add the footer shown below.
6. Save and close the document.

1997 Paid Holidays

January 1, New Year's Day, Wednesday
January 20, Martin Luther King Day, Monday
May 26, Memorial Day, Monday
July 4, Independence Day, Friday
September 1, Labor Day, Monday
November 27, Thanksgiving Day, Thursday
December 25, Christmas Day, Thursday

1998 Paid Holidays

January 1, New Year's Day, Thursday
January 19, Martin Luther King Day, Monday
May 25, Memorial Day, Monday
July 3, Independence Day Celebration, Friday
September 7, Labor Day, Monday
November 26, Thanksgiving Day, Thursday
December 25, Christmas Day, Friday

Header position:	Flush right
Header text:	Please Post
Footer position:	Flush left
Footer text:	Filename: ACT010

ACTIVITY 11

Printing

OBJECTIVES

Estimated Time: 20 minutes

- Preview a printed document
- Print full document

Your department is planning its annual picnic. You have been asked to chair this event. Write a memo asking for suggestions for food and entertainment.

INSTRUCTIONS

1. Create a new document.
2. Key the memo shown below.
3. Save the document as ACT011.
4. Preview the page to check placement and margins.
5. Enlarge the preview page.
6. Print one copy.
7. Explore the option to print more than one copy.
8. Close the document.

Current Date

Office Administration Staff

ANNUAL DEPARTMENT PICNIC

It's that time of the year when we can get away from our computers and meetings for one day! The Annual OA Picnic is scheduled for Friday, June 10.

To make this year's picnic an event to be remembered, I need your help. The department will be providing hamburgers, hotdogs, and soft drinks. For side dishes and desserts, each member is asked to bring an item to share. If your last name falls in one of the following categories, please bring one food item from that category:

> A to G, bring an appetizer
> H to N, bring a vegetable
> O to Z, bring a dessert

For entertainment, we will have the pleasure of having a repeat performance by the Rocking Rollers Band. They were a big hit last year! If you have any other ideas that you want to share, please give me a call.

Joanne Loudin
Office Manager

ACTIVITY 12

Printing

OBJECTIVES

Estimated Time: 20 minutes

- Preview a printed document
- Print full document
- Print selected text
- Print multiple copies

Send a memo announcing the winners of the annual department golf outing. In this memo, include individual winners as well as teams.

INSTRUCTIONS

1. Create a new document.
2. Key the memo on the next page.
3. Save the document as ACT012.
4. Preview the page to check placement and margins.
5. Enlarge the preview page.
6. Print two copies of document.
7. Highlight the list of winners and print one copy of the selected text.
8. Close the document.

Current Date

Advanced Technology Organization

ANNUAL GOLF OUTING

This year's annual golf outing was a big hit. We had wonderful weather and a great turnout! We gave away a ton of door prizes, too! Here are the winners:

Individual Winners:
     First Place: Rose White, Shipping
     Second Place: Barb Tietsort, Accounting
     Third Place: Ginny Wiley, Maintenance

Team Winners:
     First Place: Shipping
     Second Place: Engineering
     Third Place: Accounting

Be sure to congratulate these winners!

Courtney Jones

ACTIVITY 13

Using Cut, Paste, and Undo

OBJECTIVES

- Move text by using cut and paste
- Cancel a change by using undo

You have just returned to the office after attending "Strategies for Successful Teams," a two-day seminar. Your manager has requested that you write a report discussing the strategies of teamwork. Because you have been gone two days, work has piled up and you have limited time to write a report. You decide to compose the report at the keyboard. You know this effort will not produce a final copy the first time and that some editing will be required before you present the report to your manager.

INSTRUCTIONS

1. Create a new document.
2. Key the following report as displayed.

STRATEGIES FOR SUCCESSFUL TEAMS

Teamwork can be more effective when the following strategies are initiated within the group:

1. Each team member must have a shared sense of direction.

2. Strategies need to be clearly communicated, understood, and agreed by all.

3. Communication must be clear and direct.

4. All team members should celebrate the successes of each individual.

5. Trust and support should be encouraged individually and as a team.

6. Risk taking should be encouraged and seen as an opportunity for team growth.

We all have something to contribute, and it is up to us as individuals to decide when and how we are going to make our contributions. Becoming an effective, contributing team member takes commitment and effort. Once we decided to contribute, we will reap many rewards both as individuals and as a group!

---

3. Save the document as ACT013.
4. After keying the report, make the changes shown on the following page.

STRATEGIES FOR SUCCESSFUL TEAMS

Teamwork can be more effective when the following strategies are initiated within the group:

1. Each team member must have a shared sense of direction.

2. Strategies need to be clearly communicated, understood, and agreed by all. [handwritten: 4]

3. Communication must be clear and direct.

4. All team members should celebrate the successes of each individual. [handwritten: 6]

5. Trust and support should be encouraged individually and as a team. [handwritten: 2]

6. Risk taking should be encouraged and seen as an opportunity for team growth. [handwritten: 5]

[handwritten right margin: Rearrange & renumber]

We all have something to contribute, and it is up to us as individuals to decide when and how we are going to make our contributions. Becoming an effective, contributing team member takes commitment and effort. Once we decided to contribute, we will reap many rewards both as individuals and as a group!

[handwritten: Move second sentence before first sentence of ¶]

5. Save the revised document.

6. Explore using the undo function. Key the words "The End" at the end of the document. Use undo to remove these words.

7. Close the document.

ACTIVITY 14

Using Cut and Paste

OBJECTIVES

Estimated Time: 25 minutes

- Move text by using cut and paste

Your manager is preparing a presentation that she is planning to give to a senior journalism class at Princeton High School. She has asked you to key a draft outline of her presentation.

INSTRUCTIONS

1. Create a new document.
2. Key the information below and on the next page as displayed.

HOW TO BE A BETTER TECHNICAL WRITER

Slash Your Writing Time

1.   The first step to take once you're assigned a project.
2.   How to succeed at the critical pre-writing stage.
3.   Four mistakes that often defeat technical writers. . . and how to avoid them.
4.   An invaluable plan for identifying your reader's needs.
5.   Thirteen questions you must answer before writing the first word.
6.   How to avoid "reader overload."

Edit Documents Like A Pro

1.   The number one standard every technical writer must strive to achieve.
2.   Answering the crucial question "how long is too long"
3.   What to do about noun clumps and other reader "roadblocks."
4.   How to verbally calm a reader's fears and anxieties.
5.   Is the copy too technical? A simple test that will tell you "yes" or "no."
6.   Nine different ways you'll want to edit a technical document.

Motivate Your Audience To Read Every Word

1.   Five structural formats. . . and when to use each.
2.   Twenty-five words that absolutely don't belong in a technical document.
3.   How to test your writing's clarity.
4.   One thing every technical writer must know about using graphics.
5.   The secret to writing descriptive titles, headlines and subheads.
6.   Effectively mixing illustrations and text.
7.   Five deadly technical writing traps. . . and how to sidestep each.

Master Your Topic

1.   How to cut straight to the core of a complex topic.
2.   Eight vital information resources you should never be without.
3.   How to document your sources.
4.   When writer's block strikes--3 shortcuts to get on track.
5.   Two ways to ensure your research is comprehensive.

---

3. Save the document as ACT014.

4. Make the following changes to this document.

HOW TO BE A BETTER TECHNICAL WRITER

Slash Your Writing Time

1.   The first step to take once you're assigned a project.
2.   How to succeed at the critical pre-writing stage.
3.   Four mistakes that often defeat technical writers. . . and how to avoid them.
4.   An invaluable plan for identifying your reader's needs.
5.   Thirteen questions you must answer before writing the first word.
6.   How to avoid "reader overload."

Edit Documents Like A Pro

1.   The number one standard every technical writer must strive to achieve.
2.   Answering the crucial question "how long is too long"
3.   What to do about noun clumps and other reader "roadblocks."
4.   How to verbally calm a reader's fears and anxieties.
5.   Is the copy too technical? A simple test that will tell you "yes" or "no."
6.   Nine different ways you'll want to edit a technical document.

move this section and paste after your "motivate your audience..." section

Motivate Your Audience To Read Every Word

1.   Five structural formats. . . and when to use each.
2.   Twenty-five words that absolutely don't belong in a technical document.
3.   How to test your writing's clarity.
4.   One thing every technical writer must know about using graphics.
5.   The secret to writing descriptive titles, headlines and subheads.
6.   Effectively mixing illustrations and text.
7.   Five deadly technical writing traps. . . and how to sidestep each.

Master Your Topic

1. How to cut straight to the core of a complex topic.
2. Eight vital information resources you should never be without.
3. How to document your sources.
4. When writer's block strikes--3 shortcuts to get on track.
5. Two ways to ensure your research is comprehensive.

move this section and paste it after "Slash your writing time" section

5. Save the revised document.

6. Close the document.

ACTIVITY 15

Using Copy, Paste, and Undo

OBJECTIVES

Estimated Time: 25 minutes

• Copy text by using copy and paste
• Cancel a change by using undo

You have been a member of your organization's assessment committee for the past two years. The committee is requesting that each member develop procedures for a portfolio assessment. In organizing your thoughts for identifying the procedure, you developed the following pre-procedure questions that need to addressed. As chairperson of the committee, you developed the following form to be completed by committee members.

INSTRUCTIONS

1. Create a new document.
2. Key the document below as displayed.

Current date

All Assessment Committee Members

ASSESSMENT COMMITTEE PORTFOLIO ASSESSMENT PROCEDURES

In setting up a portfolio assessment procedure several questions need to be asked. Please complete the following form so we can compile a cohesive format for the guidelines.

1.   What is the portfolio going to assess?

2.   What knowledge and skills should the student be able to demonstrate?

3.   What guidelines on content and form will be used?

4.   How will the portfolio be evaluated?

5.   Will this be the only grade given for the course?

JANICE WHITEHOUSE

---

3. Save the document as ACT015.
4. Delete the words "assessment committee" from the subject line.
5. Use undo to cancel the change you made in the subject line.

   After keying the report, you decide to save paper by printing two reports on a page.

6. Use the copy and paste feature to copy the memo to the bottom of the page.
7. Save the revised document.
8. Close the document.

ACTIVITY 16

Using Copy and Paste

OBJECTIVES

Estimated Time: 35 minutes

+ Copy text by using copy and paste

You wish to send two letters requesting applications for employment. After creating the first letter, use copy and paste to copy repetitive parts of the letter to help create the second letter.

INSTRUCTIONS

1. Create a new document.

2. Key the document below as written.

3002 Dynamo Ct.
Clinton, OK 13032
Current Date

MargoMed Company
Human Resource Department
1000 Ivorydale Way
Mason, OH 45062

APPLICATION FORM

Please send me an application form for employment with the MargoMed Company. If you would also include an information packet about the company, I would appreciate it.

Since graduation is coming up next month, I would like to begin my job search immediately. As soon as I receive the application, it will be completed and returned. If you have any information regarding the current hiring status of administrative assistants, please let me know.

MARY LOU REXTON

---

3. Save the document as ACT016A.

You would like to send a similar letter to another company, Ohio Medical Company, 353 Technology Drive, Hamilton, OH 45022. To copy repetitive information complete the steps shown on the next page.

4. Open a new document.

5. Return to the original letter.

6. Copy the return address. Paste the address in the new document.

7. Copy and paste the body and closing of the original letter and paste it to the new document.

8. Add the inside address of the Ohio Medical Company and the company name in the first sentence.

9. Save the second letter as ACT016B.

10. Close both documents.

ACTIVITY 17

Working with Fonts and Attributes

OBJECTIVES

Estimated Time: 20 minutes

- Use a specific font
- Use bold type
- Center text

Create a flyer for your upcoming garage sale.

INSTRUCTIONS

1. Create a new document.
2. Center the first line using Times in 60 points bold.
3. Center the remaining lines in Times 24 points normal.
4. Save the document as ACT017.
5. Print one copy.
6. Close the document.

GARAGE SALE

Saturday, June 23, 1996
8044 Forest Glen Drive
9:00 a.m until 3:30 p.m.

oriental rugs
furniture
garden tools
children's toys

Everything is in excellent condition!
Everything must go!!

ACTIVITY 18   Working with Fonts and Attributes

OBJECTIVES

- Use a specific font
- Change font for specific text
- Use italic type and bold type
- Underline a word and a group of words
- Align text in the center of the page, flush left, and flush right
- Use specific point size for type

Create a flyer for an upcoming meeting of your computer users group.

INSTRUCTIONS

1. Create a new document.
2. Align the first line flush right using Times in 14 point underlined.
3. Center the next line using Univers in 36 points bold.
4. Center the remaining lines, except the last line, in Times 18 points normal.
5. Underline the word "topics" and italicize the phrase "Everyone Is Invited."
6. Align the last line flush left in Times 18 points normal.
7. Save the document as ACT018.
8. Print one copy.
9. Close the document.

<u>Please Post</u>

COMPUTER USERS GROUP

Tuesday, October 8, 1996
Conference Room C
4:00 p.m.

<u>Topics</u>
E-mail privacy
Budget for on-line services
Computer viruses

Everyone Is Invited

Call Dana Ng for additional information: Extension 6123

ACTIVITY 19

Working with Document Layout

OBJECTIVES

Estimated Time: 20 minutes

• Set specific margins
• Double space text

You are a volunteer for a community group that provides an after-school program. The fee for the program is calculated based on the family's ability to pay. Your group is always looking for donations because revenue from enrollment fees never covers the cost of the program.

You are writing a news release describing your programs needs for donations. You will use the community group's letterhead. The name of the organization appears at the top of the page, the names of the board of trustees are printed down the left side of the page, and the street address is at the bottom of the page.

INSTRUCTIONS

1. Create a new document.

2. Set your margins to coincide with the letterhead: Top, 2.5 inches, Bottom, 1.5 inches, Left, 2.5 inches, and Right, 1 inch.

3. Align the first six lines flush right.

4. Center the headline and use Univers 14 points bold.

5. Double space the body of the news release.

6. Print one copy.

7. Close the document.

News Release

August 1, 1996
FOR IMMEDIATE RELEASE
Contact: Edith G. Van Winkel
555-9480

Youngsters Need Supplies for After-School Program

The Hazelwood Community Latchkey Program is seeking donations. Needed items include all kinds of art supplies, pencils and pens, craft supplies, and paper.

"Youngsters use lots of paper, paint, crayons, and glue. We really need paper, particularly construction paper and posterboard," said program coordinator Edie Van Winkel.

In its third year, the latchkey program provides after school care for over 100 children in grades K-4. Enrollment fees are based on a family's ability to pay.

Donations may be brought to Hazelwood Elementary School anytime between 7:30 a.m. and 4:00 p.m. Arrangements can be made for pick up of your donation by calling Van Winkel at 555-9480.

Activity 19 Working with Document Layout ◆ **29**

ACTIVITY 20   Working with Document Layout

OBJECTIVES   **Estimated Time: 20 minutes**

- Set specific margins
- Add space after paragraphs
- Change orientation of page
- Set page number

Along with some colleagues, you are preparing a meeting planning notebook. Part of your contribution is to produce a page showing a sign to be hung outside of a conference room.

The sign fits into a frame on the wall outside the meeting room. The frame is designed to hold a piece of 8.5 by 11 inch paper in the landscape position. The edge of the frame covers one inch of the paper on all four sides.

This meeting room sign will be page 18 of the notebook.

INSTRUCTIONS

1. Create a new document.
2. Change the page orientation to landscape.
3. Set your margins to accommodate the frame; use a 1.5 inch on all four sides.
4. Center the name of the conference room using 24 point bold.
5. Use bold for the words "date," "time," "meeting," and "contact."
6. Add 6 points of space after each of these paragraphs.
7. Use italic type for the last paragraph.
8. Add the page number at the bottom of the page, flush right.
9. Print one copy.
10. Close the document.

West Conference Room

Date: January 21, 1997

Time: 8:30 a.m. to 3:00 p.m.

Meeting: Quality Assurance Task Force Monthly Meeting

Contact: Kirby Rosco, Extension 7881

This building is a smoke-free environment. Smoking is not permitted anywhere in the building, including this conference room.

Page 18

ACTIVITY 21   Setting Tabs

OBJECTIVES   **Estimated Time: 25 minutes**

- Clear tab settings
- Use left align tab
- Use left indent

Create a table showing world currency for various countries.

INSTRUCTIONS

1. Create a new document.
2. Center the heading
3. Clear all default tabs and set a left align tab at 4.25".
4. Set left indent at 1.5".
5. Key the document below, using the tab setting you created.
6. Save the document as ACT021.
7. Print one copy.
8. Add leaders to the tab set at 4.25". Do not include the column headings.
9. Close the document without saving your last change.

WORLD CURRENCY

Country	Monetary Unit
Argentina	Peso
Austria	Schilling
Belgium	Franc
Egypt	Pound
Finland	Mark
France	Franc
Germany	Mark
Greece	Drachma
Hong Kong	Dollar
Israel	Shekel
Italy	Lira
Japan	Yen
Netherlands	Guilder
Nigeria	Naira
Portugal	Escudo
Spain	Peseta
Sweden	Krona
Turkey	Lira
Zimbabwe	Dollar

ACTIVITY 22

Setting Tabs

OBJECTIVES

Estimated Time: 25 minutes

- Use left align tabs
- Use right align tabs
- Use decimal tabs
- Use center tabs

Create a report in tabulated format showing the estimated number of jobs supported by exports.

INSTRUCTIONS

1. Create a new document.

2. Center the three lines of the report heading.

3. Decrease right margin by .5" for the remainder of the document.

4. Clear all default tabs. Set center tabs at 2", 4", and 6". Key the column headings.

5. Set a decimal tab at 2" for second column. Set right tabs for 4.25" and 6.25" for the third and fourth columns, respectively.

6. Key the data shown.

7. Save the document as ACT022.

8. Print one copy.

9. Close the document.

Estimated Number of Jobs Supported by Exports
Selected States, 1991

(Source: Business America, March 23, 1992, pages 32-43)

State	Total Exports (In billions of $)	Manufacturing Jobs for Exports	Total Jobs for Exports
California	$58.0	360,000	725,000
Florida	$16.0	77,000	210,000
Illinois	$16.0	145,000	275,000
Louisiana	$6.5	20,000	60,000
Michigan	$21.0	155,000	270,000
New York	$31.0	150,000	350,000
Ohio	$16.0	175,000	310,000
Texas	$41.0	190,000	390,000
Washington	$29.0	71,000	142,000

ACTIVITY 23   Inserting Page Breaks

OBJECTIVES

Estimated Time: 35 minutes

- Insert a page break
- Insert page number in footer
- Suppress footer on first page

After completing research for a history report, you decide it would look better if you inserted a page break between the second and third paragraphs.

INSTRUCTIONS

1. Create a new document.
2. Use a 1.5" left and right margin.
3. Indent the first line of paragraphs 0.5".
4. Key the document below.
5. Save the document as ACT023.
6. Center the title in Times 18 points bold.
7. Double space the body text.
8. Justify the body text using Times 14 points normal.
9. Save the document.
10. Print one copy.

Henry Ford

Henry Ford was an American hero. He was a self-taught machinist and engineer whom many say changed America forever. In 1903, he founded the Ford Motor Company, a small company that manufactured automobiles.

After examining scientific management theories and studying the philosophy of efficient production as presented by Frederick Winslow Taylor, Ford changed his automobile manufacturing practices. Taylor was an efficiency expert who developed a new concept of labor that reduced the requirement for human expertise in an efficient manufacturing environment. In 1906, Ford borrowed Taylor's ideas and used them to change how his organization manufactured automobiles. Ford was the father of mass production techniques--the assembly line--which significantly changed the way people worked. Ford Motor Company not only changed the way people worked, the automobiles it manufactured changed the way people traveled.

Ford's implementation of the assembly line made automobiles affordable to the average American. His Model T, otherwise known as the Tin Lizzie, became the foremost mass-produced product in the world. Mass production became the unifying theme for American industry in the early 1900's and beyond.

The automobile revolutionized the world more than any other product until the advent of the computer. What have we learned from this lesson in history? Was Henry Ford's mass production technique really the best way to produce goods? Or are critics of the mass production philosophy correct when they point out that assembly line workers want more from a job than just being an invisible cog in the wheel of production? While the answer to these question is not an easy one, it is one we should consider carefully. We may have to make that decision about how we use computers one day!

---

11. Insert a page break before the paragraph "Ford's implementation. . ."

12. Create a footer and insert the page number. Do not print the footer on the first page.

13. Print a second copy.

14. Close the document without saving your changes.

ACTIVITY 24   Inserting Page Breaks

OBJECTIVES

Estimated Time: 40 minutes

• Insert page breaks

Create a list of 50 food items categorizing them in groups: bread and cereal group, fruit group, vegetable group, meat group, and milk group. Include ten items for each group.

INSTRUCTIONS

1. Create a new document.
2. Use 1" left and right margins.
3. Use Times 18 points bold for category titles.
4. Use Times 12 points normal for food items.
5. Insert a blank line after the last item in each category.
6. Save the document as ACT024.
7. Print one copy.
8. Insert page breaks between categories to create a separate page for each food group.
9. Print a second copy.
10. Close the document without saving changes.

ACTIVITY 25

Using Spell Checker

OBJECTIVES

Estimated Time: 30 minutes

♦ Use the spell checker

Your manager has handed you a rush job. She needs this memo by 9:00 a.m.

INSTRUCTIONS

1. Create a new document.
2. Use the simplified memorandum format and the current date. Key the memo exactly as it appears--typographical errors, misspellings, and all.
3. Save the document as ACT025.
4. Print one copy.

Martha Seibert, Marketing Director

QUALITY WRITTEN COMMUNICATION

I'm attaching a copy of an intersting article, "The Importance of Accuracy" written by Jonah A. WIse. The article appeared in this week's Communication Today magazine. I recommend each member of our department read this article and practice the techniques it offers for creating quality documents.

The article says that misspelled words and typagraphical errors hurt a company's image by projecting an "I don't cate" attitude--an attitude that says "Its not important" and "I'm too busy to do a good job." In today's competitive enviornment, our company can not afford to send out letters that aren't "letter perfect."

We must proofread our work carefully to identify isspelled words, typogrphical errors, incorrect capitalization and incorrect words usage. We've worked hard to built our customer base and they're to important to let the quality of our correspondense destroy our business relationships. I'll call you tomorrow to arrange duplication and distribution. Thank you.

Janet Coggan, Customer Service Representative

---

5. Use the speller to make the required corrections.
6. Proofread! Remember that the accuracy of your document depends not only on your ability to use the speller correctly, but on your ability to proofread your document for those errors that the speller does not highlight.
7. Print a second copy.
8. Save the revised document.
9. Close the document.

ACTIVITY 26

Using Spell Checker

OBJECTIVES

• Use the spell checker

Compose a one-page letter to your local community college requesting information about upcoming computer technology continuing education programs.

INSTRUCTIONS

1. Create a new document.
2. After composing this letter, use the spell checker to highlight misspelled words, proper nouns, and double words. Proofread to correct errors in punctuation, word usage, grammar, and content.
3. Save the document as ACT026.
4. Print one copy.
5. Close the document.

ACTIVITY 27   Replacing Text

OBJECTIVES   Estimated Time: 50 minutes

* Use the find feature to search a document for particular characters, words, or phrases
* Use the find and replace feature to replace attributes, characters, words, or phrases

INSTRUCTIONS

1. Create a new document.
2. Use the default left and right margins. Use a 1.5" top margin.
3. Key the document as displayed in standard memo format.
4. Save the document as ACT027.

DATE: Current Date

TO: Sharletta Joseph, Principal, *Coco High School*

FROM: Hai Tran, *Business Department,* Chair

SUBJECT: *Request for Approval for Entrepreneurship Class*

America is undergoing a revolution! At no other time in history has the entrepreneurial spirit of Americans been more alive. Estimates are that last year over XX new businesses were started in our community and that the number will increase by XX in the next five years. When interviewed, one entrepreneur stated his motivation to become self-employed was fueled by his company's commitment to "downsizing." A commitment that ultimately led to the elimination of his level of management. Determined never to let that happen again, this feisty ex-manager became an entrepreneur!

Historically, *Coco High School* has been a leader in supporting the employment needs of our community. We have always provided training that enables our learners to find jobs and remain as self-supporting citizens of our community. This recent increase in entrepreneurial spirit presents us with an opportunity to remain at the head of the class by offering a class in entrepreneurship that will prepare our learners not only to accept jobs, but to explore self-employment. By offering a class in *Entrepreneurship,* we will be supporting our learners, the business community, and the local economy.

As you requested, I will present an outline of the proposed Entrepreneurship curriculum and answer questions about it at Thursday's faculty meeting. This is a fine opportunity for us, Ms. Joseph. Thank you for your support.

Continued on the next page

5. Use the Find and Replace feature to make the required changes.

   - Remove italics from all proper names
   - Put all occurrences of Entrepreneurship in italics
   - Change XX to 2,000 the first time it appears
   - Change XX to 50% the second time it appears
   - Double check that entrepreneur and its derivatives are spelled correctly
   - The entrepreneur described in our memo was a woman, not a man. Be careful when you make changes! Correct any discrepancies.

6. Save the revised document.

7. Print the document.

8. Close the document.

ACTIVITY 28

Replacing Text

OBJECTIVES

Estimated Time: 50 minutes

- Use the find feature to search a document for particular characters, words, or phrases
- Use the find and replace feature to replace attributes, characters, words, or phrases

Your vice president asked you to create a one-page list of this year's sales leaders including names and addresses. You have pulled the appropriate cards from your Rolodex. Some of the cards are more than twenty years old.

INSTRUCTIONS

1. Create a new document.
2. Key the names and addresses as they appear below.
3. Save the document as ACT028.

Blaney, Joshua
3324 Lambet Circle
Manchester, Vermont 05254

Conndilaro, Courtney
1221 Nordyke Ave
Portland, Or 97208

Driver, Gertrude
305 West 30th Street
Portland, Ore 97208

Hammacher, Garnet
1318 Knotter Drive
Conway, NH 03818

Morelas, Adam
9307 Persimmon Lane
Columbia, Maryland 21045

Morris, Parker
1150 Winton Terrace
Florissant, Mo. 63031

Nieman, Oren
555 Leslie Lane
San Francisco, Ca 94120

Nobanaga, Evan
1996 Olympia Blvd.
Portland, Ore 97228

Overman, John
2077 Red Maple Court
Emeryville, Cal 94608

Peterman, Carter
128 Shellmound St
Franconia, New Hampshire 03580

Thompson, Brooke
475 Henkle Drive
Nashua, New Hampshire 03062

Westerman, Tiffany
660 Corbly Court
Cheshire Conn 06410

Zohn, Gillian
760 Manresa Lane
Burlington, Vermont 05401

---

4. Use the Find and Replace feature to make the changes to reflect current postal standards.

  ♦ Use the standard two-letter abbreviation for each state. For example, IL is used for Illinois.

  ♦ Abbreviate terms in the street address. For example, W 3rd St is preferred over West 3rd Street—no punctuation is required.

5. Save the revised document.

6. Print the document.

7. Close the document.

ACTIVITY 29   College Application Project, Part 1

OBJECTIVES   **Estimated Time: 50 minutes**

• Use a variety of word processing skills

    Applying to colleges is a major project. This is the kind of project where integrated software can simplify the process.

    Activity 29 is the first part of a four-part project. Activities 59, 79, and 98 will focus on spreadsheet, database, and integrated skills, respectively. These four activities are all part of the college application project.

INSTRUCTIONS

1. Create a new document.

2. Select at least three institutions of higher education. Choose colleges, universities, graduate schools, etc.

3. Compose and key a letter requesting an information package from one of the three institutions you selected.

4. Use your word processing skills to create the second and third letter without starting from scratch.

5. Save each letter as a separate document. Use the filenames ACT029A, ACT029B, and ACT029C.

6. Close the documents. Do not print the letters at this time.

ACTIVITY 30

Employee Benefits Project, Part 1

OBJECTIVES

Estimated Time: 60 minutes

• Use a variety of word processing skills

You are part of a team working on an employee benefits project. As you work on this project you will use many of the capabilities of an integrated software package.

Activity 30 is the first part of a four-part project. Activities 60, 80, and 99 will focus on spreadsheet, database, and integrated skills, respectively. These four activities are all part of the employee benefits project.

INSTRUCTIONS

1. Create a new document.

2. Key the memo shown on the next page. Use any word processing feature to create an attractive interesting communication. Consider using a template or wizard if your software has this kind of feature. The example shown on the next page was created by using a letterhead wizard in Microsoft Works®

3. Save your work as ACT030 and close the document.

Bright Beginnings

3552 Waycross Circle • Tucson, Arizona • Telephone (520) 555-8697

To: All Employees
From: Human Resources Department
Date: August 1, 1997
Subject: Benefits Profile

A personalized benefits profile has been developed for each Bright Beginnings employee. Your profile is attached.

The benefits profile outlines the benefits offered to Bright Beginnings employees. The programs in which you are currently enrolled are identified. Also identified are programs for which you are eligible but are not currently enrolled.

The profile includes information about the cost of your benefits—what you pay and what the company pays.

Please take time to review your benefits profile. This is an opportunity to make sure you are enrolled in the programs that are appropriate for your circumstances. It is also a good time for you to discuss benefits with your family.

The entire month of October is an open enrollment period for all benefits programs. You will have an opportunity to make changes in your benefit plan during October. The changes will become effective January 1, 1998.

A reply card is included for your use. Use this card to request information about specific benefits and the open enrollment procedures. Please complete the card and return it to the Human Resources Department by September 1, 1997.

Attachments

Bright Beginnings is an equal opportunity employer committed to a diverse workplace.

ACTIVITY 31

Fundraising Project, Part 1

OBJECTIVES

+ Use a variety of word processing skills

You are part of a team working on an fundraising project. As you work on this project you will use many of the capabilities of an integrated software package.

Activity 31 is the final activity devoted to word processing. It is also the first part of a four-part project. Activities 61, 81, and 100 will focus on spreadsheet, database, and integrated skills, respectively. These four activities are all part of the fundraising project.

INSTRUCTIONS

1. Create a new document.

2. Key the newsletter shown on the next two pages. Use any word processing feature to create an attractive interesting communication. Consider using a template or wizard if your software has this kind of feature. The example show on the next two pages was created by using a newsletter wizard in Microsoft Works®.

3. Save your work as ACT031 and close the document.

NEWSLINE

RAMSEYCOMMUNITYCENTER   SUMMER 1998

From the Heart

A gift from the heart is a special gift. This year you are being asked to give a gift from your heart.

The Ramsey Community Center serves hundreds individuals and families--your family and your For some, it is lifestyle activities such as softball, aerobics, or summer camp. For others, it is a lifeline for eldercare, emergency food, or social services.

Whatever your situation, the Ramsey Community Center has an impact on your life. And, more than likely, touches your heart. Your gift can be directed toward your special concerns and interests.

For the first time, this year your gift can be earmarked for one of the four areas: programs, social services, staff development, and community outreach programs.

This year, please consider a gift from the heart.

For additional information, please contact the Ramsey Community Center Development Office at (201) 555-

151 CLAYTONAVENUE   RAMSEY, NJ 07446

Your Gift Means . . .

Your gift means so much to so many.

For a woman caring for her elderly father, it means one afternoon a week for herself while her dad participates in an eldercare program.

♥

For a young family it means affordable daycare while the father works and the mother attends college.

♥

For a 35-year old man with arthritis it means exercise all winter in a heated swimming pool..

♥

1998 Goal Set At $125,00

"The campaign has only just begun, and already we are a third of the way there," according to volunteer campaign director Susan Szwed.

Early gifts from generous corporate sponsors of equal 36 per cent of this year's goal of $125,000.

Giving levels for the *from the heart* campaign have been established for corporations and individuals. The include corporate sponsor, $5,000; corporate patrons, $1,000; individual sponsors, $500; and individual $100.

"We expect to raise another $35,000 from the business community and $45,000 from individuals," said Szwed. "This is a very generous community and the Ramsey Center plays a vital role here," she added.

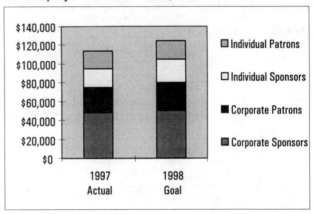

ACTIVITY 32

Entering and Saving Data

OBJECTIVES

Estimated Time: 15 minutes

- Enter text into several cells
- Use Undo function
- Save a file

You are a member of a golf tournament and have been asked to provide a list of people who will be playing. It is expected that more people will enter the tournament as the tournament date approaches. You decide to enter the list in a spreadsheet making it easier to enter changes as the roster grows.

INSTRUCTIONS

1. Create a new spreadsheet.

2. Key the data shown below as displayed. As you complete each entry, experiment with ways to move the cursor (e.g. TAB, arrow keys, and ENTER).

3. Replace *Apple* in cell B3 with **Peach**. Use the Undo feature to change the name back to *Apple*.

4. Save the spreadsheet as ACT032.

5. Close the file.

	A	B	C	D
1	Duffer's Golf Tournament Roster			
2	First Name	Last Name	Street Address	
3	Jonathan	Apple	17 N. Cobbler	
4	Lloyd	Copas	1648 Glensprings Drive	
5	Vickie	Ingels	4890 King Court	
6	Annette	Janson	781 White Avenue	
7	Clancy	Lopez	6241 Knight Court	
8	Jack	Nickels	7777 Washington Blvd.	
9	Mary Ellen	O'Hearn	113 Stillwater Path	
10	Renee	Pomeroy	6791 Hollister Road	
11	Chang	Tseng	1623 Whispering Winds	
12	Stanford	Underwood	10 New Bluff Road	
13	Glen	Voss	567 Main	

ACTIVITY 33   Entering and Saving Data

OBJECTIVES   **Estimated Time: 15 minutes**

- Enter text into several cells
- Save a file
- Close the spreadsheet

Your chemistry class is starting to study the periodic table. You are using the spreadsheet to keep a list of the element names, atomic numbers, and symbols.

INSTRUCTIONS

1. Create a new spreadsheet.

2. Key the data below as displayed. As you complete each entry, experiment ways to move the cursor (e.g. TAB, arrow keys, and ENTER).

3. Save the spreadsheet as ACT033.

4. Close the file.

	A	B	C
1	Element	Atomic #	Symbol
2	Hydrogen	1	H
3	Helium	2	He
4	Lithium	3	Li
5	Beryllium	4	Be
6	Boron	5	B
7	Carbon	6	C
8	Nitrogen	7	N
9	Oxygen	8	O
10	Fluorine	9	F

ACTIVITY 34

Using Save As

OBJECTIVES

Estimated Time: 15 minutes

* Save files
* Save an existing file with a different name

You are required to turn in a monthly expense report to your supervisor. You want to set up a spreadsheet that you can reuse without overwriting data from a previous month. You have decided to create a master worksheet, then save it under a different name at the beginning of each month.

INSTRUCTIONS

1. Create a new spreadsheet.
2. Key the data shown below as displayed.
3. Save the file as ACT034.
4. Save the file as EXPJAN.
5. Save the file as EXPFEB.
6. Save the file as EXPMAR.

	A	B	C	D	E
1		Week 1	Week 2	Week 3	Week 4
2	Travel				
3	Lodging				
4	Meals				
5	Misc.				
6					
7	Totals				

ACTIVITY 35

Editing Cells

OBJECTIVES

Estimated Time: 20 minutes

* Use backspace key
* Edit cell entries

You are researching the development of the car before the year 1900. As you research, you want to be able to add information to your findings.

INSTRUCTIONS

1. Create a new spreadsheet.

2. Key the text shown below as displayed. As you enter the text, use the backspace key to correct errors.

3. From your research, you find that the Ford's top speed was 21 miles per hour. Go to cell D5 and add the text **top speed, 21 m.p.h.** after the words "2 cylinder."

4. You also found that the Benz had a horsepower of 1.5. Key **1.5 h.p.** in cell D4 after the words "1 cylinder."

5. Save the file as ACT035.

6. Close the file.

	A	B	C	D
1	Model	Year	Country	Description
2	Daimler	1886	Germany	1 cylinder
3	Daimler	1896	Germany	2 cylinder
4	Benz	1888	Germany	1 cylinder
5	Ford	1896	USA	2 cylinder
6	Renault	1898	France	2.25 h.p.

ACTIVITY 36   Editing Cells/Inserting Rows

OBJECTIVES   **Estimated Time: 20 minutes**

* Edit cell entries
* Insert a row
* Save an edited entry

Your store is doing a demographic study of the community. You are responsible for recording the findings in a spreadsheet.

INSTRUCTIONS

1. Create a new spreadsheet.

2. Key the data shown below as displayed.

3. Save the spreadsheet as ACT036.

4. Edit the cell with the year 2000 to read **2000 (Projected)**.

5. You decide to add the following two lines before the Population Income section:

   Population Average Age
       33.5   33.0   33.4

6. Save the file.

7. Close the file.

	A	B	C	D
1		1980	1990	2000
2	Population By Race			
3	White	9,482	9,377	9,358
4	Black	8,259	9,386	10,015
5	Hispanic	3,566	5,612	6,836
6	Asian	1,997	3,743	4,474
7	Population By Gender			
8	Female	12,263	14,557	15,796
9	Male	11,041	13,561	14,887
10	Population Income			
11	Average	15,497	24,205	28,912
12	Per Capita	5,958	9,284	10,974

ACTIVITY 37

Inserting Rows

OBJECTIVES

Estimated Time: 20 minutes

- Insert blank rows
- Add additional data

You own The Suntan Hut and have recently added a new sunscreen product to your price list. You prefer to insert this new product in the list in such a way as to maintain a logical order. To add the product, you need to insert a blank row.

INSTRUCTIONS

1. Create a new spreadsheet.
2. Key the data shown below as displayed.
3. Move to cell A4.
4. Insert a new row at row four.
5. In cell A4 key **Bronzer SPF 5**.
6. In cell B4 key **9.00**.
7. In cell C4 key **8.50**.
8. In cell D4 key **7.50**.
9. Save the file as ACT037.
10. Close the file.

	A	B	C	D	E
1					
2	Product	Qty 1 Price	Qty 10 Price	Qty 25 Price	
3	Bronzer SPF 3	8.95	7.95	6.95	
4	Bronzer SPF 8	9.95	8.95	7.95	
5	Bronzer SPF 15	10.45	9.79	8.50	
6	Bronzer SPF 18	11.00	9.50	7.00	

ACTIVITY 38

Inserting Columns

OBJECTIVES

Estimated Time: 15 minutes

- Insert blank columns
- Add additional data

You use a worksheet to list your personal expenses for each month. After you key the column headings for the twelve months, you realize that it would be helpful to total expenses by quarter.

INSTRUCTIONS

1. Create a new spreadsheet.

2. Key the data shown below as displayed. Continue listing the months through December in row 2.

3. Insert a new column between the existing columns D and E.

4. In cell E2 key Q1.

5. Save the file as ACT038.

6. Close the file.

	A	B	C	D	E
1					
2	Expense	Jan	Feb	Mar	Apr
3	Rent				
4	Equipment				
5	Utilities				
6	Payroll				
7					

ACTIVITY 39   Working with Rows and Columns

OBJECTIVES   **Estimated Time: 30 minutes**

- Change column width
- Insert rows
- Move data

You decide to use a spreadsheet to keep track of the costumes owned by the drama club.

INSTRUCTIONS

1. Create a new spreadsheet.

2. Key the data shown below.

3. Change the column widths of each column to fit the content.

4. Save the file as ACT039.

Costume	Size	Condition	Date Checked
Belly dancer	Misses 8	Fair	4/30/95
Boy's nightshirt	Adult S	Good	6/1/94
Boy's nightshirt	Adult S	Good	6/1/94
Boy's nightshirt	Adult M	Excellent	6/1/94
Captain Hook	Adult M	Good	6/1/94
Court jester	Adult S	Poor	4/30/95
Lederhosen	Adult S	Fair	4/30/95
Lederhosen	Adult M	Fair	4/30/95
Peter Pan	Adult S	Poor	6/1/94
Phantom of the Opera	Adult M	Excellent	4/30/95
Princess	Misses 10	Good	12/1/94
Toreador	Adult M	Good	4/30/95
Tuxedo	Men 40 Reg	Fair	9/10/95
Tuxedo	Men 42 Reg	Fair	9/10/95
Tuxedo with tails	Men 42 Long	Poor	9/10/95
Wedding Gown	Misses 4	Poor	9/10/95
Wedding Gown	Misses 10	Fair	9/10/95
Wedding Gown	Misses 12	Excellent	9/10/95
Wendy	Misses 6	Good	6/1/94
Witch	Misses 10	Excellent	4/30/95

Continued on the next page

5. Add the costumes from the *Wizard of Oz,* shown below, at the bottom of the spreadsheet

6. The first twenty costumes are in alphabetical order. Add rows in the appropriate locations and move the Wizard of Oz costumes so that the entire list is in alphabetical order.

7. Change column widths to fit content if necessary.

8. Save and close the file.

Costume	Size	Condition	Date Checked
Dorothy	Misses 6	Excellent	Current Date
Scarecrow	Adult L	Excellent	Current Date
Tin Man	Adult L	Excellent	Current Date
Lion	Adult L	Excellent	Current Date
Wizard of Oz	Adult S	Excellent	Current Date

ACTIVITY 40

Printing a Spreadsheet

OBJECTIVES

Estimated Time: 20 minutes

- Center a spreadsheet on the printed page
- Print a spreadsheet

You are using a spreadsheet to keep track of the statistics for a little league team. The coach would like you to bring the statistics you have been keeping to the game. You need to print the spreadsheet.

INSTRUCTIONS

1. Key the data shown below.

2. Adjust the page set up so that the spreadsheet prints in the center of the page.

3. Save the file as ACT040.

4. Print the file.

5. Close the file.

	A	B	C	D	E
1	Last Name	First Name	At Bats	Hits	RBI
2	Alverez	Marcia	17	6	3
3	Clark	Susan	21	9	7
4	Daniels	Frank	19	6	2
5	Peters	Rose	21	8	9
6	Reeves	Lance	12	4	0
7	Ryan	Norman	18	9	3
8	Stevens	Chris	16	7	1
9	Topazio	Janet	16	5	2
10	Tsai	Ming	20	8	4
11	Vidas	Petros	22	10	5
12	Webber	James	17	7	2

ACTIVITY 41

Printing a Spreadsheet

OBJECTIVES

Estimated Time: 30 minutes

• Print a spreadsheet

You have been asked to print a list of the ten movies which have earned the most revenues at the box office.

INSTRUCTIONS

1. Create a new spreadsheet.

2. Key the data shown below as displayed.

3. Save the spreadsheet as ACT041.

4. Print the spreadsheet.

5. Close the spreadsheet.

	A	B	C	D
1	Top Ten Movies			
2	Total Revenues			
3				Revenue
4	Movie Title		Year	in Millions
5				
6	E.T.		1982	228
7	Star Wars		1977	194
8	Return of the Jedi		1983	168
9	Batman		1989	151
10	Empire Strikes Back		1980	142
11	Home Alone		1990	140
12	Ghostbusters		1984	138
13	Jaws		1975	130
14	Raiders of the Lost Ark		1981	116
15	Indiana Jones		1984	109

ACTIVITY 42

Using Print Preview

OBJECTIVES

Estimated Time: 20 minutes

• Preview a spreadsheet before printing

The local chamber of commerce wants to increase tourism. You are on a committee to monitor attendance figures at some local attractions. These figures will be used to help decide a course of action for future promotions.

INSTRUCTIONS

1. Create a new spreadsheet.

2. Key the data shown below.

3. Save the file as ACT042.

4. Use print preview to see how the printed page will look without actually printing it.

5. Change the page orientation from portrait to landscape. Select print preview to view the changed orientation.

6. Make other adjustments, if necessary, to fit all the data on a single page. For example, you might need to change the width of some columns.

7. Save your changes.

8. Print the spreadsheet.

9. Close the file.

	A	B	C	D	E	F	G	H	I	J	K	L	M
1	Attraction Attendance Figures												
2		Jan	Feb	Mar	Apr	May	Jun	Jul	Aug	Sep	Oct	Nov	Dec
3	Zoo	64014	57784	63784	78195	81322	172150	272781	251211	146786	135005	96899	133914
4	Museum	34420	31711	32378	33949	33171	31221	30788	29925	27755	26967	26115	30156
5	Park	0	0	0	0	501489	814997	1225921	1172396	869071	408934	0	0

ACTIVITY 43

Printing a Range

OBJECTIVES

Estimated Time: 30 minutes

♦ Print a range of data

As a teacher's assistant, you are keeping the grades for a biology class. By keeping the information in a spreadsheet, you can print out only the data the teacher requests.

INSTRUCTIONS

1. Create a new spreadsheet.

2. Key the information shown below.

3. The teacher requests the grades for Hatcher. Print the range of grades for Hatcher; include Hatcher's full name.

4. The teacher also wants a list of the names of students in the class. Print the range of both last names and first names.

5. Save the file as ACT043.

6. Close the file.

	A	B	C	D	E	F	G	H
1	Biology Grades							
2	Last	First	Quiz 1	Quiz 2	Mid-term	Quiz 3	Project	Final
3	Abanto	Juanita	95	90	97	95	87	93
4	Abrams	Laetitia	90	95	93	90	86	87
5	Baldrick	Glen	85	80	89	80	92	84
6	Christie	James	85	85	88	100	82	90
7	Cook	Rodger	90	90	94	95	86	97
8	D'Adamo	Crystal	75	85	92	90	80	87
9	Fields	Tamera	95	100	97	100	97	95
10	Harris	Robert	95	95	93	90	91	91
11	Hatcher	Jeanette	90	95	96	95	88	100
12	Horwitz	Aaron	100	95	97	95	95	95
13	Kinney	Sheila	85	95	94	80	86	91
14	McCaw	Chris	70	75	81	80	81	85
15	Meece	Henry	90	90	97	95	89	92
16	Reed	Paul	80	85	91	95	79	89
17	Schwartz	Janet	85	85	93	95	80	84
18	Stockton	Mark	90	95	88	95	87	88
19	Strauss	Lisa	80	85	90	90	91	86

ACTIVITY 44

Creating Headers and Footers

OBJECTIVES

Estimated Time: 20 minutes

- Create a header
- Create a footer

At the conclusion of each day, you need to print a report that shows the number of customer service calls you have handled over the telephone each hour. The report must show your name at the top center, the current date at the bottom left, and the current time at the bottom right of each page.

INSTRUCTIONS

1. Create a new spreadsheet.

2. Key the data shown below.

3. Create a header that includes your first and last name in the top center of the page.

4. Create a footer that prints the current date flush left and the current time flush right.

5. Save the spreadsheet as ACT044.

6. Close the file.

	A	B	C
1	Customer Service Call Log		
2			
3	Hour	# of Calls	
4	9:00 a.m.	22	
5	10:00 a.m.	18	
6	11:00 a.m.	14	
7	12:00 p.m.	24	
8	1:00 p.m.	31	
9	2:00 p.m.	17	
10	3:00 p.m.	15	
11	4:00 p.m.	12	
12	5:00 p.m.	16	

ACTIVITY 45

Inserting Page Breaks

OBJECTIVES

Estimated Time: 30 minutes

• Insert page breaks into a spreadsheet
• Print column heading on each page

Your company has three stores in the metropolitan area — north, south, and midtown. You wish to print a separate report for each store without specifying three separate print ranges and issuing the print command three times.

INSTRUCTIONS

1. Create a new spreadsheet.

2. Key the data shown below.

3. Save the spreadsheet as ACT045.

4. Insert a page breaks before cells A5 and A8.

5. Freeze the column titles so they will print at the top of the column on each page. In other words, row 1 will print at the top of all three pages.

6. Create a header using the text "Business Activity Report."

7. Create a footer including a page number and the current date.

8. Print the spreadsheet.

9. Save your work and close the spreadsheet.

	A	B	C	D	E	F
1		Mon	Tue	Wed	Thu	Fri
2	North					
3	Sales	100	94	114	120	88
4	Rentals	45	65	71	23	44
5	Midtown					
6	Sales	98	77	62	45	59
7	Rentals	44	39	38	49	55
8	South					
9	Sales	122	133	146	99	152
10	Rentals	87	78	56	62	99

ACTIVITY 46   Formatting Numbers and Text

OBJECTIVES

Estimated Time: 30 minutes

- Use the dollar number format
- Change the size and style of specific text
- Change the font

You are comparing prices between two grocery stores. You price several items you use regularly. You can then determine which store has, on average, the better prices.

INSTRUCTIONS

1. Create a new spreadsheet.

2. Enter the data shown below. Spell out all words in column A; do not abbreviate.

3. Save the spreadsheet as ACT046.

4. Format the prices using the dollar format. Adjust column widths to fit content.

5. Change the appearance of the text in column A; use 14 points bold

6. Change the font for the entire spreadsheet; use Univers.

7. Save your work and print the spreadsheet.

8. Close the file.

	A	B	C
1		Store #1	Store #2
2	Celery	1.35	1.33
3	Milk	2.56	2.59
4	Bread	.99	.99
5	Eggs	.95	.98
6	Tom. Soup	.63	.65
7	Dish Soap	2.39	2.45
8	Tuna	1.15	.99
9	O. Juice	1.05	.99
10	P. Butter	2.49	2.39
11	Sand. Bags	1.99	1.99
12	Froz. Pizza	2.99	2.95

ACTIVITY 47   Formatting Numbers and Text

OBJECTIVES   **Estimated Time: 30 minutes**

- Add commas to the number format
- Use italics
- Center text over more than one column

You are doing a report on the ecosystems of the world's largest deserts. You are keeping some information in a spreadsheet.

INSTRUCTIONS

1. Create a new spreadsheet.

2. Enter the data shown below.

3. Save the spreadsheet as ACT047.

4. Format the area of the deserts using commas. Adjust column widths to fit content.

	A	B	C
1	The Largest Deserts		
2	Name of Desert	Area (sq. mi.)	
3	Sahara	3500000	
4	Gobi	500000	
5	Great Victoria	250000	
6	Gibson	250000	
7	Rub'al-Khali	235000	
8	Kalahari	225000	

5. Add a column so you can insert the location, by continent, of each desert. Enter the appropriate continent next to the desert. Adjust the column width to fit content.

6. Change the size and font of the content of A1. Center the text in A1 over all three columns.

7. Change the appearance of the names of the deserts; use italics.

8. Save your work and print the spreadsheet.

9. Close the file.

Location by continent
Africa: Kalahari, Sahara
Asia: Gobi, Rub'al-Khali
Australia: Gibson, Great Victoria

ACTIVITY 48   Formatting Numbers and Text

OBJECTIVES   **Estimated Time: 30 minutes**

* Use the decimal format
* Use the percentage format
* Change the number of decimal places shown

   You are preparing a report for a driver's education class. In a spreadsheet, you have compiled a list of reasons for accidents.

INSTRUCTIONS

1. Create a new spreadsheet.

2. Enter the data shown below. The data are percentages expressed in decimals.

3. Adjust column widths to fit content.

4. Save the spreadsheet as ACT048.

5. Copy the data from column B to columns C and D.

6. Change the number of decimal places shown to two for data in column C.

7. Change the number format for the data in column D to percentage. Change the number of decimal places shown in the percentage format to one. (Example: 22.7%)

8. Adjust column widths to fit content.

9. Save your work and print the spreadsheet.

10. Close the file.

	A	B	C	D
1	Causes for Accidents			
2		Percent		
3	Speed	0.122		
4	Failed to yield	0.151		
5	Passed stop sign	0.02		
6	Disregarded signal	0.035		
7	Drove left of center	0.018		
8	Improper overtaking	0.013		
9	Made improper turn	0.045		
10	Followed too closely	0.055		
11	Other	0.227		
12	No apparent cause	0.314		

ACTIVITY 49   Working with Formulas

OBJECTIVES   **Estimated Time: 20 minutes**

+ Use autosum
+ Write a multiplication formula

You are a member of a volunteer fire department. You have a booth in a week-long festival. From this booth, money is raised by selling T-shirts, hats, bumper stickers, and mugs that promote the fire department. You record the number of items sold each day in a spreadsheet.

INSTRUCTIONS

1. Create a new spreadsheet.

2. Enter the data shown below. Adjust column widths to fit content.

3. Save the spreadsheet as ACT049.

4. Calculate the total number of shirts sold during the week using the autosum feature. Autosum adds all the numbers in a specified range.

5. Calculate the total quantity for each of the other items: hats, stickers, and mugs.

	A	B	C	D	E	F
1		T-shirts	Hats	Stickers	Mugs	
2	Monday	31	18	14	16	
3	Tuesday	28	15	9	11	
4	Wednesday	37	17	11	8	
5	Thursday	33	19	6	13	
6	Friday	29	22	10	9	
7	Saturday	46	37	19	18	
8						
9	Total Quantity					
10	Unit Price					
11	Gross Sales					

6. Enter the unit prices for each item: T-shirts, $13; Hats, $7; Stickers, 50¢; and Mugs, $3. Adjust number of decimal places if necessary.

7. Calculate the gross sales for each item; multiply the quantity times the unit price. Adjust column widths and decimal places if necessary.

8. Use autosum to calculate the total gross sales in cell F11. Add a box around the total.

9. Save your work and print the spreadsheet.

10. Close the file.

ACTIVITY 50   Working with Formulas

OBJECTIVES   **Estimated Time: 20 minutes**

* Write a subtraction formula
* Write a division formula

    You have returned from a trip. You kept track of your odometer readings between fill-ups and the number of gallons each fill-up required. You use a spreadsheet to calculate the number of miles driven and the miles per gallon for your car.

INSTRUCTIONS

1. Create a new spreadsheet.

2. Enter the data shown below.

3. Save the spreadsheet as ACT050.

4. In cell C3, enter the formula to calculate the number of miles driven. Copy the formula to cells C4 to C11.

5. In cell E3, enter the formula to calculate miles per gallon (mileage divided by gallons). Copy the formula to cells E4 to E11.

6. Change number format in columns D and E to display two decimal places.

7. Save your work and print the spreadsheet.

8. Close the file.

	A	B	C	D	E	F
1	Miles Per Gallon					
2	Beginning	Ending	Mileage	Gallons	Miles Per Gallon	
3	32156	32345		9.7		
4	32345	32581		11.9		
5	32581	32798		10.4		
6	32798	33007		10.3		
7	33007	33216		10.75		
8	33216	33420		10.2		
9	33420	33653		10.9		
10	33653	33871		11		
11	33871	34074		9.9		

ACTIVITY 51

Working with Formulas

OBJECTIVES

Estimated Time: 45 minutes

- Use autosum
- Write a multiplication formula with mixed references
- Write an addition formula
- Copy a formula

You are planning an awards banquet for your company. The CEO has not decided who will attend. If she invites only the sales team, it will be approximately 125 people. The management group would add another 50 people and there are about 125 customer service representatives. You have put together a menu of the CEO's favorite foods. You are using a spreadsheet to show the cost per person and the total cost depending on the number of guests.

INSTRUCTIONS

1. Create a new spreadsheet.

2. Enter the data shown below. Save the spreadsheet as ACT051.

	A	B	C	D	E
1	Menu	Per Person	Number of persons		
2			125	175	300
3	Coquille St. Jaques	$ 5.50	$ 687.50	$ 962.50	$ 1,650.00
4	Mixed Greens with Raspberry Vinaigrette	included			
5	Mesquite Grilled Breast of Free Range Chicken	16.50	2,062.50	2,887.50	4,950.00
6	New Potatoes with Parsley and Butter	included			
7	Steamed Broccoli with Hollandaise	included			
8	Tuxedo Torte	4.25	531.25	743.75	1,275.00
9	Choice of Coffee, Decafe, or Tea	no charge			
10					
11	Food Total				
12	Gratuity	18%	18%	18%	18%
13					
14					
15	Sales Tax	6.5%	6.5%	6.5%	6.5%
16					
17	Total				

Continued on the next page

3. In cell B11, calculate the cost per person. In cell B13, calculate the gratuity. In cell B15, calculate the sales tax. (In the state where the dinner will be held, the gratuity is taxable.) In cell B17, calculate the total cost per person.

4. Adjust column widths and number of decimal places. The final total should be formatted for currency. Save your work.

5. In cell C3, enter a formula to calculate the cost of the appetizer for 125 persons. Write the formula using mixed references (relative and absolute) so that the formula can be copied to calculate the appetizer for 175 and 300 persons. You will also want to copy the formula to calculate the three cost levels for the entree and dessert.

6. Adjust column widths and number of decimal places. Save your work.

7. Copy the formulas for the food total, gratuity, tax, and total.

8. Save your work and print the spreadsheet.

9. Before closing the file, experiment with different numbers of guests.

10. Close the file without saving your changes.

ACTIVITY 52

Using @ Functions

OBJECTIVES

Estimated Time: 45 minutes

- Write a formula using the AVERAGE function
- Write a formula using the MAX function
- Write a formula using the MIN function

The semester has come to a close and you need to compute the averages of each student's total test scores. You would also like statistics showing the highest, lowest, and average scores for each test.

INSTRUCTIONS

1. Create a new spreadsheet.

2. Key the data shown on the following page.

3. Save the spreadsheet as ACT052. Save your work often.

4. In cell E4 write a formula containing a function to average Reta's three test scores.

5. Copy the formula in E4 to E5 through E9.

6. In cell B11 write a formula containing a function that will determine the highest (maximum) score for Test 1.

7. Copy the formula in B11 to C11 through E11.

8. In cell B12 write a formula containing a function that will determine the lowest (minimum) score for Test 1.

9. Copy the formula in B12 to C12 through E12.

10. In cell B13 write a formula containing a function that will determine the average score for Test 1.

11. Copy the formula in B13 to C13 through E13.

12. Format the averages for zero decimal places.

13. Save your work and print the spreadsheet.

14. Close the file.

	A	B	C	D	E
1	Test Score Results				
2					
3	Student	Test 1	Test 2	Test 3	Avg.
4	Reta	94	100	70	
5	Paige	76	72	72	
6	Bill	82	70	96	
7	Angie	78	90	72	
8	Jeff	96	74	90	
9	Gail	66	72	70	
10					
11	High				
12	Low				
13	Average				

ACTIVITY 53

Using @ Functions

OBJECTIVES

Estimated Time: 15 minutes

• Use the TODAY function
• Use the SUM function

You own a small lawn service called **New Leaf Lawn Care**. You want to create an invoice system using your spreadsheet software. You will create a template that can be used to prepare each invoice.

INSTRUCTIONS

1. Create a new spreadsheet.

2. Key the data shown below. Use the formatting displayed for text, alignment, and borders.

3. Every time you open the invoice file, you want it to display today's date. Enter the function that displays the current date in cell D4.

4. In cell D17, enter the formula to sum the range D7 through D16.

5. Save the spreadsheet as ACT053.

6. Print the spreadsheet.

7. Close the file.

	A	B	C	D
1	Invoice			
2	New Leaf Lawn Care			
3				
4			Date:	
5				
6	Description			Amount
7				
8				
9				
10				
11				
12				
13				
14				
15				
16				
17			Total:	
18				

ACTIVITY 54

Using @ Functions

OBJECTIVES

Estimated Time: 15 minutes

• Use the PAYMENT function

You are getting ready to buy a car. You are comparing several cars. You want to use the spreadsheet to calculate your monthly payment depending on car cost and interest rate.

INSTRUCTIONS

1. Create a new spreadsheet.

2. Key the data shown below as displayed.

3. Save the spreadsheet as ACT054.

4. In cell C5, use the payment function to determine the monthly payment. The number format should be dollar with zero decimal places.

5. Change the interest rate to 7.5% and notice the change in payment.

6. Change the cost of car to $9,000 and notice the change of payment.

7. Save your work and print the spreadsheet.

8. Close the file.

	A	B	C
1	Cost of Car		$11,000
2	Interest Rate		9.00%
3	No. of Payments		48
4			
5	Payment		

ACTIVITY 55 — Creating a Chart

OBJECTIVES

Estimated Time: 15 minutes

- Create a pie chart

You are researching the continents. You have prepared a list of the continents and the area in square miles for each continent.

INSTRUCTIONS

1. Create a new spreadsheet.
2. Key the data shown below as displayed. Adjust column widths as necessary.
3. Save the spreadsheet ACT055.
4. Create a pie chart with the continent names as labels.
5. Save your work.
6. Print the pie chart.
7. Close the chart and spreadsheet.

	A	B
1	**Continent**	**Area**
2	Africa	11,678,000
3	Antarctica	5,400,000
4	Asia	17,005,000
5	Australia	2,967,900
6	Europe	4,069,000
7	North America	9,351,000
8	South America	6,885,000

ACTIVITY 56

Creating a Chart

OBJECTIVES

Estimated Time: 15 minutes

- Create a pie chart
- Add a title to a chart

You asked a random group of customers which flavor of ice cream they prefer. You will create a pie chart showing the results.

INSTRUCTIONS

1. Create a new spreadsheet.
2. Key the data shown below.
3. Save the spreadsheet and chart as ACT056.
4. Create a pie chart from the range A3 through B8.
5. Add the following title to your chart: **Flavor Preferences**
6. Save your work.
7. Print the chart.
8. Close the chart and spreadsheet.

	A	B	C
1	Ice Cream Survey		
2			
3	Flavor	Number	
4	Vanilla	38	
5	Chocolate	22	
6	Strawberry	15	
7	Peppermint	10	
8	Rocky Road	5	

ACTIVITY 57

Editing a Chart

OBJECTIVES

Estimated Time: 25 minutes

* Change from one chart type to another
* Use a description on a chart axis

You are doing research on the increase of pollution in the world. You have found statistics for the countries that produce the most garbage per person per year.

INSTRUCTIONS

1. Create a new spreadsheet.

2. Key the data shown below.

3. Create a pie chart without labels.

4. Save the spreadsheet and chart as ACT057.

5. Change the pie chart to a horizontal bar chart.

6. Add the title, **Country**, to the X-axis.

7. Add the title, **Pounds Per Person**, to the Y-axis.

8. Save your work and print the chart.

9. Close the chart and spreadsheet.

	A	B	C	D	E
1	Country	Pounds per person per annum			
2	U.S.	1,905			
3	Canada	1,378			
4	Finland	1,111			
5	Norway	1,043			
6	Denmark	1,034			

ACTIVITY 58

Editing a Chart

OBJECTIVES
          Estimated Time: 30 minutes

- Change from one chart type to another
- Add a title to an existing chart

You are planning a camping trip to Europe next summer. As you are making your plans, you decide to research the average rainfall of several cities to see which has the least rain during the summer months and which month might be the best one for travel.

INSTRUCTIONS

1. Create a new spreadsheet.

2. Key the data shown below.

3. Save the spreadsheet as ACT058.

4. Create a bar chart from the data.

5. You notice that the bar chart is hard to read so create a line chart with data points. Use the Y-axis for the amount of rainfall and the X-axis for the months. Each city will be represented by a different line.

6. Use a legend to make the chart easier to understand.

7. Set the Y-axis for a minimum value of 0 and a maximum value of 90.

8. Save your work.

9. Key in the following for a title:

   Average Rainfall of European Cities

   (In Millimeters)

10. Save your work and print the chart.

11. Close the file.

	A	B	C	D	E	F
1	Average Rainfall of European Cities (In Millimeters)					
2		May	Jun	Jul	Aug	Sep
3	Athens	15	5	5	5	15
4	Berlin	60	70	80	70	50
5	London	45	50	40	50	55
6	Paris	50	50	55	60	50
7	Rome	35	20	5	35	75

ACTIVITY 59   College Application Project, Part 2

OBJECTIVES   **Estimated Time: 30 minutes**

• Use a variety of spreadsheet skills

    Applying to colleges is a major project. This is the kind of project where integrated software can simplify the process.

    Activity 59 is the second part of a four-part project. Activities 29, 79, and 98 focus on word processing, database, and integrated skills, respectively. These four activities are all part of the college application project.

INSTRUCTIONS

1. Create a new spreadsheet.

2. Select at least four institutions of higher education.

3. Enter cost data for each institution. For each school, calculate the yearly total for each component. Sample data are shown below and on the next page.

4. Save your work as ACT059. (If you decide to use more than one spreadsheet, name them ACT059A, ACT059B, etc.)

5. Create 3-D pie charts for each institution to show the relationship among the cost components. Sample chart is shown on next page.

6. Save your work often.

7. Create a stacked bar graph showing the total yearly cost of each school.

8. Print the portion of the spreadsheet showing the data for one institution, include the data used to calculate the yearly totals for each component.

9. Print the pie chart and the data used to create it for one institution. Select the same institution you used in item 8.

10. Print the four-school cost comparison data and chart. Sample chart is shown on next page.

11. Close all charts and spreadsheets.

	A	B	C	D	E	F	G
1	Institution A						
2	Tuition	6,000	per semester	2	semesters	12,000	per year
3	Room & Board	5,000	per semester	2	semesters	10,000	per year
4	Books	250	per semester	2	semesters	500	per year
5	Transportation	800	airline ticket	3	trips	2,400	per year
6	Total					24,900	

Continued on the next page

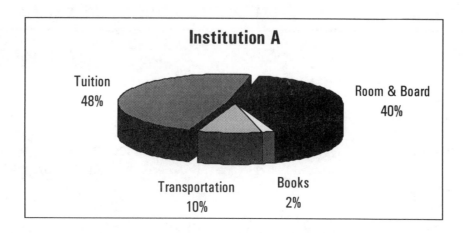

Institution A

Tuition 48%

Room & Board 40%

Transportation 10%

Books 2%

	A	B	C	D	E
1	Cost Comparison				
2	Institution	A	B	C	D
3	Tuition	12000	22000	15000	5600
4	Room & Board	10000	0	8400	5000
5	Books	500	500	1050	700
6	Transportation	2400	2400	1600	1800
	Total	24900	24900	26050	13100

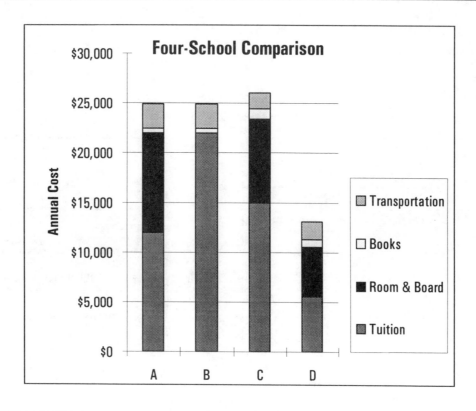

Four-School Comparison

Annual Cost

$30,000
$25,000
$20,000
$15,000
$10,000
$5,000
$0

A B C D

Transportation
Books
Room & Board
Tuition

ACTIVITY 60   Employee Benefits Project, Part 2

OBJECTIVES   **Estimated Time: 30 minutes**

• Use a variety of spreadsheet skills

You are part of a team working on an employee benefits project. As you work on this project you will use many of the capabilities of an integrated software package.

Activity 60 is the second part of a four-part project. Activities 30, 80, and 99 focus on word processing, database, and integrated skills, respectively. These four activities are all part of the employee benefits project.

INSTRUCTIONS

1. Create a new spreadsheet.

2. Enter data for participation in selected benefit programs shown below.

3. Save your work as ACT060A.

4. Create 3-D bar chart to show the level of eligibility, enrollment, and participation in the three benefit programs. Sample chart is shown below.

5. Save your work often.

6. Enter data for employee and employer contributions to selected benefit programs shown on the next page.

7. Save your work as ACT060B.

8. Create bar chart that compares the employee and employer contributions for selected benefit programs. Sample chart is shown on next page.

9. Save and print your work.

10. Close both spreadsheets and charts.

	A	B	C	D
1		Employees	Employees	Employees
2		Eligible	Enrolled	Participating
3	Dental	380	157	124
4	Health	380	211	196
5	401(k)	380	186	186

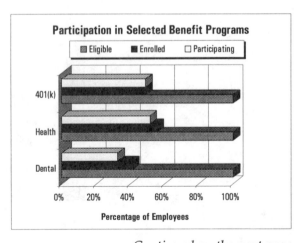

Continued on the next page

	A	B	C
1		Contribution	
2		Employer	Employee
3	Pension	100%	0%
4	Life Insurance	100%	0%
5	Health Insurance	90%	10%
6	Dental Insurance	60%	40%
7	401(k)	33%	67%

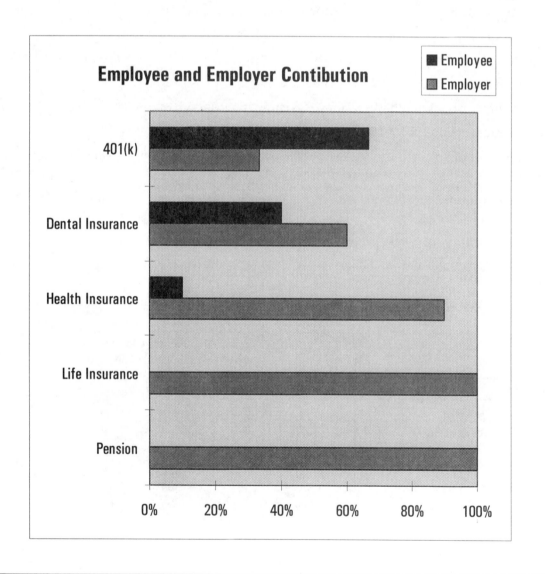

Employee and Employer Contibution

ACTIVITY 61   Fundraising Project, Part 2

OBJECTIVES   **Estimated Time: 30 minutes**

• Use a variety of spreadsheet skills

    You are part of a team working on an fundraising project. As you work on this project you will use many of the capabilities of an integrated software package.

    Activity 61 is the final activity devoted to spreadsheets. It is also the second part of a four-part project. Activities 31, 81, and 100 focus on word processing, database, and integrated skills, respectively. These four activities are all part of the fundraising project.

INSTRUCTIONS

1. Create a new spreadsheet.

2. Enter fundraising campaign data shown below, include results for 1997 and goals for 1998.

3. Save your work as ACT061A.

4. Create a stacked column chart to show contributions for 1997 and projections for 1998.

5. Save your work often.

6. Enter data for tracking the 1997 and 1998 campaigns shown on the next page.

7. Save your work as ACT061B.

8. Create two stacked column charts to show progress of the 1997 and 1998 campaigns. A sample of the 1997 chart is shown on the next page.

9. Create a column chart that shows the percentage of goal achieved by July 1998, September 1998, and November 1998.

10. Save and print your work.

11. Close both spreadsheets and charts.

	A	B	C
1		1997 Actual	1998 Goal
2	Corporate Sponsors	48,000	50,000
3	Corporate Patrons	27,000	30,000
4	Individual Sponsors	20,000	25,000
5	Individual Patrons	19,000	20,000
6	Total	114,000	125,000

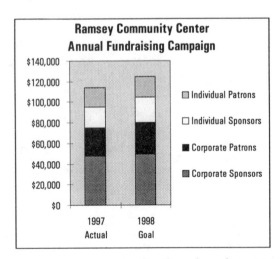

Continued on the next page

A	B	C	D
Campaign Progress, 1997			
	1997 July	1997 September	1997 November
Corporate Sponsors	28000	36000	48000
Corporate Patrons	2000	21000	27000
Individual Sponsors	0	14000	20000
Individual Patrons	0	8800	19000
Total	30000	79800	114000
Campaign Progress, 1998			
	1998 July	1998 September	1998 November, Projected
Corporate Sponsors	39000	55000	55000
Corporate Patrons	6000	27000	30000
Individual Sponsors	0	18500	25000
Individual Patrons	0	11700	20000
Total	45000	112200	130000

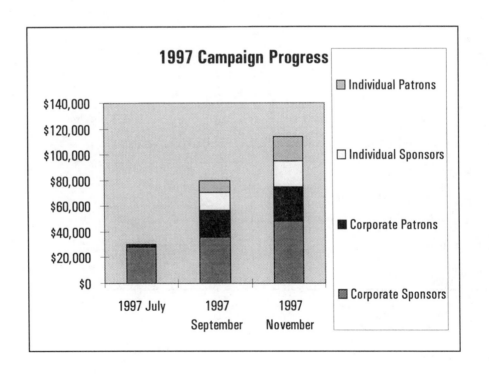

ACTIVITY 62

Creating a Record

OBJECTIVES

- Create a form
- Enter data using a form
- View a database as a list
- Save a database

You volunteer at the local library several afternoons each week. Recently, a patron has donated several cartons of books to the library. The librarian has asked you to make a list of all the books that were donated so he can determine which books will be kept and which will be offered to other libraries. You decide to create a database of information about these books.

INSTRUCTIONS

1. Create a new database; name it ACT062.

2. Create a data entry form using the fields shown below.

Title:
Subtitle:
Author name, last:
Author name, first:
Copyright year:
ISBN:

3. Enter the data for the first book, shown below, in the first record.

4. Save your work.

5. View the database as a list.

6. Return to the form view and print the database.

7. Close the database.

Title:	Death of Common Sense, The
Subtitle:	How Law Is Suffocating America
Author name, last:	Howard
Author name, first:	Philip
Copyright year:	1994
ISBN:	0-679-42994-8

ACTIVITY 63　　　　　　　　　　　　　　　Creating a Record

OBJECTIVES　　　　　　　　　　　Estimated Time:　15 minutes

+ Create a form
+ Enter data using list view
+ View a database using a form
+ Save a database

　　You have decide to put your personal address book in a database. You want to create a sample before you enter all the data.

INSTRUCTIONS

1.　Create a new database; name it ACT063.

2.　Create a data entry form using the fields shown below.

Last name:
First name:
Street address:
City:
State:
Zip Code:
Telephone:

3.　Change to the list view and enter the sample data, shown below, in the first record.

4.　Save your work.

5.　View the database using a form.

6.　Print the database.

7.　Close the database.

Last name:　　　Becker
First name:　　　Donna
Street address:　2008 Crystal Parkway
City:　　　　　　Chapel Hill
State:　　　　　North Carolina
Zip Code:　　　27514
Telephone:　　(Leave this field blank—you do not have the current number.)

ACTIVITY 64

Editing a Record

OBJECTIVES

Estimated Time: 15 minutes

- Edit a record
- Save changes to database

You are tracking your grades for your ten-week current events class using a database

INSTRUCTIONS

1. Create a new database; name it ACT064.

2. Create a data entry form using the fields shown below. You might have to abbreviate the names of some of the fields.

3. Enter the grades for each activity.

Quiz 1:	81
Quiz 2:	72
Editorial:	85
Letter to Editor:	80
Test 1:	83
Quiz 3:	77
Campaign Project:	92
Quiz 4:	90
Book Report:	85
Final Exam	87

4. Save your work.

5. Correct the score on Quiz 3; the correct score is 87.

6. Change the field name Qwiz 4 to Test 2.

7. Save your work and print the database.

8. Close the database.

ACTIVITY 65

Editing a Record

OBJECTIVES

Estimated Time: 15 minutes

• Edit a record
• Save changes to database

You decide to make some changes to your address book database.

INSTRUCTIONS

1. Open the database ACT063. (If you have not completed Activity 63, do so now and then continue with this activity.)

2. Use Donna Becker's given first name—Veldonna.

3. Use the two-digit postal abbreviation for North Carolina—NC.

4. Add the telephone number in the correct field—(910) 555-4891.

5. Save your work and print the database.

6. Close the database.

ACTIVITY 66

Adding and Deleting Records

OBJECTIVES

Estimated Time: 15 minutes

• Add records to a database
• Delete a record from a database

In this activity you will begin a project for your chemistry class. Your teacher has asked you to key some of the elements from the periodic table into the first field of a new database. Your class is taking an alphabetic approach to studying chemical elements; this week you are learning the elements with names that begin with the letter A.

INSTRUCTIONS

1. Create a new database; name it ACT066.

2. Create a data entry form using the fields shown below.

Element:
Symbol:
Atomic Number:
Discovery Date:

---

3. Enter the data for the first element, shown on the next page, in the first record.

4. Create a second record and enter the data for the second element.

5. Continue to create records and enter data for the remaining elements shown on the next page.

6. Save your work.

7. Return to the first record and review your work one record at a time. Check each of the eight records using the form view.

8. Delete the record for Barium.

9. View the database as a list to make sure the record for Barium has been deleted.

10. Print the database as a list.

11. Close the database.

Element:	Symbol:	Atomic Number:	Discovery Date:
Actinium	Ac	89	1899
Aluminum	Al	13	1827
Americium	Am	95	1944
Antimony	Sb	51	
Argon	Ar	18	1894
Arsenic	As	33	1250
Astatine	At	85	1940
Barium	Ba	56	1808

ACTIVITY 67   Adding and Deleting Records

OBJECTIVES

Estimated Time: 15 minutes

• Add records to a database
• Delete records from a database

In this activity you will create a database of famous Greek mathematicians for your mathematics class.

INSTRUCTIONS

1. Create a new database; name it ACT067.

2. Create a data entry form using the fields shown below.

Mathematician:
Birth Date:
Country:

---

3. Enter the data for the first mathematician, shown on the next page, in the first record.

4. Create a second record and enter the data for the second mathematician.

5. Continue to create records and enter data for the remaining mathematicians shown on the next page.

6. Save your work.

7. Return to the first record and review your work one record at a time. Check each of the eight records using the form view.

8. Delete the records for Avicenna, Descartes, Euclid, and Newton—they are not Greek.

9. View the database as a list to make sure the three records have been deleted.

10. Print the database as a list.

11. Close the database.

Mathematician:	Birth Date:	Country:
Appollonius	262 BCE	Greece
Archimedes	287 BCE	Greece
Aristotle	384 BCE	Greece
Avicenna	980 CE	Arabia
Descartes	1596 CE	France
Euclid	300 BCE	Greece
Euler	1701 CE	Switzerland
Newton	1642 CE	England
Plato	428 BCE	Greece
Ptolemy	100 CE	Greece
Pythagorus	580 BCE	Greece

ACTIVITY 68

Working with Fields

OBJECTIVES

Estimated Time: 30 minutes

- Create additional fields
- Set field width
- Add data to records
- Change field width

You are creating a database of information about various organizations concerned with animals in your community.

INSTRUCTIONS

1. Create a new database; name it ACT068.

2. Create a data entry form and enter the data shown below. Use the default for the width of the fields.

Organization:	Area Code	Telephone:
Animal Rescue Funds, Inc.	312	555-4053
Animal Rights Community of Greater Chicago	312	555-6810
Cook County SPCA	312	555-6100
League of Animal Welfare	312	555-8122
Midwestern Wildlife Center	708	555-6650
Save the Animal Foundation	312	555-8321
Scratching Post Shelter	312	555-2287

3. Change the widths of the fields to fit the content.

4. Create additional fields for the information that shown on the next page. Set the width of each field to accommodate the longest entry in the list. (You do not have the zip code for any of the addresses. Create a zip code field so it will be available when you get the information.)

5. Save your work.

6. Print the record for the Scratching Post Shelter.

7. Close the database.

Organization	Address	City	State	Zip Code
Animal Rescue	2077 Daly Ave	Chicago	IL	
Animal Rights	566 Scott St	Chicago	IL	
Cook County SPCA	8400 Lincoln Hwy	Chicago	IL	
League of Animal	9770 E Wacker Blvd	Chicago	IL	
Midwestern Wildlife	3010 Walnut St	Oak Brook	IL	
Save the Animal	8000 Lakeshore Dr	Chicago	IL	
Scratching Post Shelter	315 Willis Way	Chicago	IL	

ACTIVITY 69

Working with Fields

OBJECTIVES

Estimated Time: 30 minutes

- Move field
- Format a field
- Delete a field

You have been asked to create a database for your sales force goals and sales.

INSTRUCTIONS

1. Create a new database; name it ACT069.

2. Create a data entry form and enter the data shown below. Set the width of the fields to fit content.

3. Save you work.

Representative	Quarter Sales	Years of Service	Rep Number	Quarter Goal
Akbar, Naila	6413.00	14	82-012	6500.00
Ch'ien, Hsi	5841.58	10	86-001	5500.00
Gwinnett, Charles	6328.56	1	95-002	6000.00
Isaacs, Aaron	5991.57	4	92-013	6000.00
Galdos, Benito	6256.03	8	88-008	6000.00
Golightly, Ellie	7050.10	17	79-004	4500.00
Stokes, TaNisha	6005.20	6	90-025	5500.00
Thayer, Diana	7000.10	1	95-007	8000.00

4. Move the rep number field so that it appears in the first column in the list view.

5. Delete the years of service field. Delete the data in this field.

6. Save your work and print the database as a list.

7. Close the database.

ACTIVITY 70

Working with Fields

OBJECTIVES

Estimated Time: 30 minutes

- Edit a field name
- Format a field for a date
- Format a field for time

As part of an internship as an events coordinator for a community recreation center, you are creating a database of special events to be held at during 1997. You are working from notes left by the previous intern.

INSTRUCTIONS

1. Create a new database; name it ACT070.

2. Create, name, and set the width for five fields. The field name for the first field is Activity. Use appropriate names for the other fields

3. Enter the data shown below.

4. Use a date format for the date field.

5. Use a time format for the time fields.

6. Save you work.

Activity	Details	
Dance	Friday, February 14	Starts at 7:30 p.m. and ends at 11:30
Easter Egg Hunt	Saturday, March 29	Begins at 10:30 and ends at noon
Art Show	Sunday, May 4	Opens at 1 p.m. and closes at 5:00.
Fireworks	Friday, July 4	Starts at 9 and ends at 10:30
Hayride	Saturday, October 4	Starts at 5:00 and ends at 9 p.m.
Halloween Party	Friday, October 31	6 to 8 p.m.

7. Change the field name from Activity to Special Event.

8. Save your work and print the database as a list.

9. Close the database.

ACTIVITY 71

Sorting a Database

OBJECTIVES

Estimated Time: 30 minutes

• Sort a database using one field
• Sort a database using multiple fields

You are reviewing the outstanding invoices for your family's business. You are interested in seeing which invoices are the oldest and which are for the greatest amounts.

INSTRUCTIONS

1. Create a new database; name it ACT071.

2. Create, name, and set the width for four fields. Suggested field names are shown below.

3. Format the date field to show the name of the month, a two-digit day, and a four-digit year.

4. Format the amount field as currency, including the dollar sign and two decimals.

5. Format the invoice number field to display five digits, including the leading zeros.

6. Enter the data for each record.

7. Save you work.

Customer	Amount	Invoice No.	Invoice Date
Atme	$ 150.00	00122	May 30, 1997
Atme	$ 150.00	00236	June 23, 1997
Coldton	$1,700.00	00102	May 28, 1997
Coldton	$ 200.00	00103	May 28, 1997
Coldton	$1,100.00	00172	June 06, 1997
Davot	$ 500.00	00101	May 27, 1997
Davot	$ 500.00	00171	June 05, 1997
Felton	$2,000.00	00157	June 04, 1997
Felton	$ 200.00	00208	June 13, 1997
Oldter	$ 100.00	00092	April 25, 1997
Zyko	$1,000.00	00237	June 23, 1997
Zyko	$ 450.00	00311	July 02, 1997

8. Sort the database by the amount field while viewing record as forms. You want the record with the largest balance due to be your first record. Browse the records to see the new order.

9. Change to list view and make sure the records are in order with the largest balance first and the smallest balance last.

10. Save your work and print the database as a list.

11. Sort the database so the records are in order by date and then by invoice number. You want the record with the oldest date to appear first and the record with the most recent date to appear last. If there is more than one invoice with the same date, you want them to appear in order by invoice number.

12. Save your work and print the database as a list.

13. Close the database.

ACTIVITY 72

Searching a Database

OBJECTIVES

Estimated Time: 30 minutes

- Search the next record
- Search all records

You are reviewing the outstanding invoices for your family's business. You are interested in seeing which invoices are the oldest and which are for the greatest amounts.

INSTRUCTIONS

1. Open the database ACT071. (If you have not completed Activity 71, do so now and then continue with this activity.)

2. View the records in the database as forms.

3. Use find or search (not query) to find the next record for the customer named Atme.

4. Still viewing records as forms, use find or search to find all the records for the customer named Atme. Browse the records that you find.

5. Switch to list view and print a list of the records you found.

6. Show all records while still in list view.

7. Find the next record for the customer named Coldton. Repeat this step and find each of the records for the customer named Coldton.

8. Still viewing records as a list, use find or search to find all the records for the customer named Coldton.

9. Print the list of the records you found.

10. Show all records and save your work.

11. Close the database.

ACTIVITY 73

Finding and Replacing Data

OBJECTIVES

Estimated Time: 30 minutes

• Find and replace data in database records

You are creating a database that contains information about the demonstration models displayed in your friend's computer store. After creating the database, you will update it with some new information when some of the demo equipment is upgraded.

INSTRUCTIONS

1. Create a new database; name it ACT073.

2. Create, name, and set the width for six fields. Suggested field names are shown below.

3. Save you work.

Brand	Hard Drive	RAM	Mouse	Monitor	Modem
Dyno	420 MG	8 MG	Yes	14"	No
Dyno	420 MG	8 MG	Yes	15"	Yes
Dyno	540 MG	8 MG	Yes	14"	No
Dyno	540 MG	8 MG	Yes	15"	Yes
Supero	850 MG	16 MG	Yes	15"	No
Supero	850 MG	16 MG	Yes	17"	Yes
Stratos	1 GIG	16 MG	Yes	17"	Yes
Stratos	1 GIG	32 MG	Yes	17"	Yes

4. All of the Dyno computers are being replaced to meet new requirements, and all the monitors will be 17 inches. Use find and replace to update the database with the information shown below.

5. Save your work.

6. View the database as a list and print the list.

7. Close the database.

	Find	Replace with
Hard Drive	420 MG	540 MG
RAM	8 MG	16 MG
Monitor	14″ and 15″	17″

ACTIVITY 74

Querying a Database

OBJECTIVES

Estimated Time: 30 minutes

• Create a query using a single criterion

For your drama class, you are creating a database of 1990-1994 plays that won New York Drama Critics' Circle Awards. You will include the name of each play, the season, and information about which plays won Pulitzer Prizes.

INSTRUCTIONS

1. Create a new database; name it ACT074.

2. Create, name, and set the width for three fields. Suggested field names are shown below.

3. Save you work.

Season	Play	Pulitzer Prize
1993-94	*Three Tall Women*	Yes
1993-94	*Twilight: Los Angeles, 1992*	No
1992-93	*Angels in America: Millennium Approaches*	Yes
1992-93	*Someone Who'll Watch Over Me*	No
1992-93	*Kiss of the Spider Woman*	No
1991-92	*Dancing at Lughnasa*	No
1991-92	*Two Trains Running*	No
1990-91	*Six Degrees of Separation*	No
1990-91	*Our Country's Good*	No
1990-91	*The Will Rogers Follies*	No
1990-91	*A Room of One's Own*	No

4. Create a query to find all plays in the database that won a Pulitzer Prize. The single criterion used in the query is Yes for the Pulitzer Prize field.

5. View the results of your query as a list and print the list.

6. Close the database.

ACTIVITY 75

Querying a Database

OBJECTIVES

Estimated Time: 30 minutes

• Create a query using multiple criteria

On September 1, 1997 you are asked to telephone some customers with past due accounts. Before you begin this project, you decide to organize the accounts to determine which calls to make first.

INSTRUCTIONS

1. Create a new database; name it ACT075.

2. Create, name, and set the width for the first five fields. Suggested field names are shown below.

3. Create a sixth field that calculates the number of days past due. Use a formula that subtracts the due date from today's date (September 1, 1997).

4. Save you work.

Account No.	Contact	Balance	Due Date	Today's Date	Days Past Due
444-2991-93	Tom Mattes	$3,356.21	July 16, 1997	Sept. 1, 1997	
444-5290-94	Sandi Wills	$1,223.96	July 2, 1997	Sept. 1, 1997	
444-6204-94	Carol Luis	$1,500.01	July 9, 1997	Sept. 1, 1997	
445-2334-93	Angela De Fazio	$6,808.88	June 3, 1997	Sept. 1, 1997	
445-9292-93	Joshua Culnen	$2,057.29	May 3, 1997	Sept. 1, 1997	
488-0084-91	Tiffany Cisneros	$1,500.25	June 1, 1997	Sept. 1, 1997	
488-1001-92	Hans Jaeger	$120.05	May 04, 1997	Sept. 1, 1997	
488-2077-92	Bruce Rusconi	$1,499.22	May 28, 1997	Sept. 1, 1997	
488-3552-91	Karen Lee	$1,500.00	May 30, 1997	Sept. 1, 1997	
488-4576-91	Diego Martin	$1,501.00	July 3, 1997	Sept. 1, 1997	
488-7609-91	Deron Williams	$2,089.91	July 1, 1997	Sept. 1, 1997	

5. Create a query to find all the accounts that are 60 days or more past due.

6. Print the results of this query as a list.

7. Create another query to find all the accounts that are both more than 90 days past due and have a balance of more than $2,000.

8. Print the results of this query as a list.

9. Close the database.

ACTIVITY 76

Querying a Database

OBJECTIVES

Estimated Time: 30 minutes

• Create a query using a range

You are working in the human resources department of a large corporation. The company is about to offer early retirement packages to employees who will be 55 by December 31, 1997. You need to query the database to determine who is eligible. Before querying the entire database, you decide to use 15 records as a practice run.

INSTRUCTIONS

1. Create a new database; name it ACT076.

2. Create, name, and set the width for the fields needed to enter the data shown below.

3. Enter the data shown below and save your work.

Last Name	Employee ID	Birth Year
Abrams	276-629	1951
Acombs	357-864	1977
Adams	531-301	1949
Adams	642-471	1932
Adleta	474-084	1956
Albers	510-232	1952
Alexander	753-951	1954
Allen	951-951	1942
Amshoff	852-175	1958
Anderson	548-977	1945
Ando	111-985	1964
Arnsperger	113-002	1943
Asher	560-963	1938
Auteri	192-837	1972
Ayvazian	425-791	1953

4. Create a query to find the employees who will be 55 by December 31, 1997. Before writing the query, calculate what year employees were born if they turn 55 in 1997.

5. Your supervisor is pleased with your work, but there is some additional information to consider. Employees who will be 62 by December 31, 1997 will need additional information about social security benefits. These employees will not be included in your target group.

6. Change your query to find employees who will be at least 55 but who will not yet be 62 by December 31, 1977.

7. Print the results of this query as a list.

8. Close the database.

ACTIVITY 77

Generating a Report

OBJECTIVES

• Generate and run a report

You decide to create a database of technical terms for your mechanics class. You also want to create a glossary of terms by generating a report from your database.

INSTRUCTIONS

1. Create a new database; name it ACT077.

2. Create, name, and set the width for the fields needed to enter the data shown below.

3. Enter the data shown below and save you work.

Term	Mechanical Area	Definition
Agate	Printing	1/14 inch; column measure
Ampere	Electronics	potential difference of 1 volt across 1 ohm
Board foot	Lumber Milling	144 cubic inches
Bolt	Textile Milling	40 yards
Btu	Electronics	1 lb. water 1 degree Fahrenheit
Decibel	Electronics	smallest sound change human ear hears
Ell	Textile Milling	1/32 bolt
Gross	Manufacturing	12 dozen
Hertz	Electronics	cycles per second

4. Generate and run a report;

   a. use a single column report.

   b. include only the Term and Definition fields.

   c. do NOT sort the report.

   d. accept the default presentation style.

   e. use "Glossary" as the title of your report.

5. View the report on your screen.

6. Save the report as REPORT77.

7. Print the report.

8. Close the report and the database.

ACTIVITY 78

Generating a Report

OBJECTIVES

Estimated Time: 30 minutes

• Generate and run a report

You are creating a database of important plays by Tennessee Williams for your literature class. You need to create a report that shows the name of each play and whether or not it won a New York Drama Critics' Circle Award (NYDCC).

INSTRUCTIONS

1. Create a new database; name it ACT078.

2. Create, name, and set the width for the fields needed to enter the data shown below.

3. Enter the data shown below and save your work.

Play	Year	Pulitzer	NYDCC
The Glass Menagerie	1944	No	Yes
A Streetcar Named Desire	1947	Yes	Yes
Camino Real	1953	No	No
Cat on a Hot Tin Roof	1955	Yes	Yes
Suddenly Last Summer	1958	No	No
Sweet Bird of Youth	1959	No	No

4. Generate and run a report;

    a. use a single column report.

    b. include only the Play and NYDCC fields.

    c. do NOT sort the report.

    d. accept the default presentation style.

    e. use "NYDCC Status" as the title of your report.

5. View the report on your screen.

6. Save the report as REPORT78.

7. Print the report.

8. Close the report and the database.

ACTIVITY 79

College Application Project, Part 3

OBJECTIVES
Estimated Time: 45 minutes

• Use a variety of database skills

    Applying to colleges is a major project. This is the kind of project where integrated software can simplify the process.

    Activity 79 is the third part of a four-part project. Activities 29, 59, and 98 focus on word processing, spreadsheet, and integrated skills, respectively. These four activities are all part of the college application project.

INSTRUCTIONS

1. Open a new database and name it ACT079A.

2. Create a database for tracking information about colleges. See samples of data fields on the next page.

3. Create a record for each college to which you are interested in applying.

4. Generate and print a report of all schools to which you have applied.

5. Generate and print a report of all schools in the database and their application deadline. Sort the report by the deadline date.

6. Open a second database and name it ACT079B.

7. Create a database for financial aid and scholarship information. See samples of data fields on the next page.

8. Generate a report for all financial aid and scholarship programs for which you are qualified. Sort the report by the application date deadline.

9. Save your work and close all open files.

Sample data fields for ACT079A:

Name of institution
Street Address
City
State
Zip Code
Date application requested
Date application received
Date application completed
Date application mailed
Application deadline
Planned visit
Date visited
Tuition
Room and Board
Notes

Sample data for ACT79B

Name of institution or organization
Street Address
City
State
Zip Code
Date application requested
Date application received
Qualified
Date application completed
Date application mailed
Essay required
Essay completed
References required
References contacted

ACTIVITY 80

Employee Benefits Project, Part 3

OBJECTIVES

Estimated Time: 45 minutes

♦ Use a variety of database skills

You are part of a team working on an employee benefits project. As you work on this project you will use many of the capabilities of an integrated software package.

Activity 80 is the second part of a four-part project. Activities 30, 60, and 99 focus on word processing, spreadsheet, and integrated skills, respectively. These four activities are all part of the employee benefits project.

INSTRUCTIONS

1. Open a new database and name it ACT080A.

2. Create a database of benefits available to employees. See data below.

3. Create a record for each benefit program.

4. Generate and print a report of all programs available to employees with less than one year of service. Sort the data by the name of the program.

5. Open a second database and name it ACT080B.

6. Create a database of employee information. See data on the next page.

7. Create a record for each employee.

8. Generate a report that shows all information for an employee. Use the title "Personal Profile." Print a report for only one employee.

9. Save your work and close all open files.

Benefit	First day of Eligibility	Single	Single Plus One	Family	Payroll Deduction
Dental	31	0	Not Available	11	Yes
Health	31	28	54	74	Yes
Life	1	0	Not Available	Not Available	No
Pension	366	0	Not Available	Not Available	No
Vision	91	2	Not Available	15	Yes
Fitness Center	1	12	Not Available	50	Yes

Continued on the next page

Name	Employee ID	Birthdate	Employ Date	Dental	Health	Life	Pension	Vision	Fitness Center
Putnam	85-9110	2/16/52	11/1/90	Single	Single	Yes	Yes	No	No
Qadri	23-2367	10/22/53	5/1/88	Family	No	Yes	Yes	No	Single
Qayoumi	84-0823	6/18/60	8/1/88	Family	Single+1	Yes	Yes	Single	Family
Quan	68-5635	2/17/51	2/1/92	Single	Family	Yes	Yes	No	Single
Quinn	36-7843	10/14/71	2/1/93	Single	Family	Yes	Yes	Single	No
Racadio	73-3544	7/2/49	8/1/88	Family	No	Yes	Yes	Family	Single
Randolph	62-3656	1/3/64	2/1/94	Family	Family	Yes	Yes	No	Single
Ransom	77-4709	1/8/58	8/1/89	Single	No	Yes	Yes	Family	No
Reckers	66-1053	3/27/36	6/1/90	Single	Single	Yes	Yes	Single	Single
Reed	55-4227	3/30/70	8/1/90	Family	Family	Yes	Yes	No	Family
Requardt	77-5468	3/11/65	4/1/92	No	No	Yes	Yes	No	No
Reynolds	79-1825	5/21/45	2/1/92	Family	Family	Yes	Yes	Single	No
Rice	58-6381	5/3/39	4/1/91	No	Family	Yes	Yes	No	No
Rikas	56-6672	6/18/55	3/1/91	Single	Single+1	Yes	Yes	Single	Family
Rno	22-7610	7/11/59	7/1/95	Family	Family	Yes	Yes	Family	Single

ACTIVITY 81

Fundraising Project, Part 3

OBJECTIVES

Estimated Time: 45 minutes

+ Use a variety of database skills

You are part of a team working on an fundraising project. As you work on this project you will use many of the capabilities of an integrated software package.

Activity 81 is the final activity devoted to databases. It is also the third part of a four-part project. Activities 31, 61, and 100 focus on word processing, spreadsheet, and integrated skills, respectively. These four activities are all part of the fundraising project.

INSTRUCTIONS

1. Open a new database and name it ACT081.

2. Create a database for pledges and donations. See data below.

3. Create a record for each donor shown below. (In order to save time and space, only selected fields are included.)

4. Generate and print a report of all pledges and gifts over $1,000. Sort the data by size of gift.

5. Generate and print a report of corporate sponsors. Sort the report by zip code.

6. Generate and print a report of any donation or pledge from an address outside New Jersey.

7. Save your work and close all open files.

Donor Name	Address	City	State	Zip Code	Pledge	Gift	Level of Giving
Cash, Jameson	3018 Pinter Cir	Dover	DE	19903	500	0	Individual Sponsor
Colton Manufacturing Co.	5400 Oxford Ave	Ramsey	NJ	07446	1000	1000	Corporate Patron
Depenbrock, Reginald	8550 Hickory Ln	Ramsey	NJ	07446	500	500	Individual Sponsor
Firestone, Connor	216 Home St	Ramsey	NJ	07446	100	100	Individual Patron
Haluk, Jonathan	6145 Lytham Ct	Ramsey	NJ	07446	100	0	Individual Patron
Herbst, Geoffrey	3290 Appleton Dr	Ramsey	NJ	07446	100	100	Individual Patron
Hetzel, John	940 Bridle Ln	Ramsey	NJ	07446	100	100	Individual Patron
Hural Laboratories, Inc.	8195 Twig Ave	Ramsey	NJ	07446	5000	5000	Corporate Sponsor
Julian, Sharon	3911 Fox Trail	Ramsey	NJ	07446	500	500	Individual Sponsor
Kineaster & Arness, LLP	2505 Oak St	Ramsey	NJ	07446	5000	2500	Corporate Sponsor
McCabe, Eileen	611 Paxton Dr	Ramsey	NJ	07446	100	100	Individual Patron
New Jersey Chimes, Inc.	400 Walnut St	Teaneck	NJ	07666	15000	5000	Corporate Sponsor
Newfield Group, Inc.	3638 Walter St	Secaucus	NJ	07094	1000	1000	Corporate Patron
Ott, Dennis	1124 Green Ln	Ramsey	NJ	07446	100	100	Individual Patron
Windser, DeAnne	2662 Britton Pl	Ramsey	NJ	07446	500	500	Individual Sponsor

ACTIVITY 82

Inserting Clip Art

OBJECTIVES

Estimated Time: 20 minutes

• Insert clip art

Your department is planning its annual picnic. You have been asked to chair this event. Create a flyer to remind everyone about the picnic and what they are supposed to bring.

INSTRUCTIONS

1. Create a new document.

2. Set the top margin at 2 inches. Set left, right, and bottom margins at 1 inch.

3. Key the text shown below. Center the text and use Times in 18 point. Use uppercase, italics and bold as shown below.

4. Save the document as ACT082.

5. Increase the size to 24 points for the all text except the words continuous performances and the information about the bring-a-dish.

6. Preview the page to check placement and margins.

7. Insert a piece of clip art somewhere on the page. Select a piece of art that is appropriate for a picnic.

8. Save you work and print one copy.

9. Close the document.

Office Administration Staff

ANNUAL DEPARTMENT PICNIC

Friday, June 10
3 to 9 p.m.

Rocking Rollers Band
Continuous Performances

Bring-A-Dish
Appetizers and Snacks: Last names begin with **A thru G**
Vegetables and Salads: Last names begin with **H to N**
Desserts: Last names begin with **O thru Z**

ACTIVITY 83

Inserting Clip Art

OBJECTIVES

Estimated Time: 20 minutes

• Insert clip art

You have been asked to print a list of the ten movies which have earned the most revenues at the box office through 1990.

INSTRUCTIONS

1. Create a new spreadsheet.

2. Key the data shown below as displayed.

3. Save the worksheet as ACT083.

4. Insert clip art related to movies. Position the art above the second and third column.

5. Save your work and print the worksheet.

6. Close the worksheet.

	A	C	D
1	Top Ten Movies		
2	Total Revenues		
3			Revenue
4	Movie Title	Year	in Millions
5			
6	E.T.	1982	228
7	Star Wars	1977	194
8	Return of the Jedi	1983	168
9	Batman	1989	151
10	Empire Strikes Back	1980	142
11	Home Alone	1990	140
12	Ghostbusters	1984	138
13	Jaws	1975	130
14	Raiders of the Lost Ark	1981	116
15	Indiana Jones	1984	109

ACTIVITY 84

Inserting Clip Art

OBJECTIVES

Estimated Time: 20 minutes

+ Insert clip art

You decide to add clip art to a database form that was created in a previous activity.

INSTRUCTIONS

1. Open the database ACT071. If you have not completed Activity 71, do so now and then follow the remaining instructions.

2. Select any record in the database and view the database form.

3. Insert a piece of clip art somewhere on the page. Move and size the art so that it is compatible with the rest of the form.

4. Save your work as ACT084.

5. Browse other records in the database and see that the art appears on the form for each record.

6. Select any record and print just that record as a form. The art will appear on the printout.

7. Close the database.

ACTIVITY 85   Drawing and Inserting Art

OBJECTIVES   **Estimated Time: 30 minutes**

- Draw an object
- Group objects
- Ungroup objects
- Regroup objects
- Add color to an object
- Insert a frame in a document
- Copy a group of objects

You want to create some simple art that you can use on a series of documents to tie them together.

INSTRUCTIONS

1. Create a new file.

2. Draw a 2" x 2" square. Measurements can be approximate.

3. Draw a rectangle that measures 2" long and ¼" wide.

4. Duplicate the rectangle.

5. Position the three elements as shown below.

6. Group the elements and move them to the middle of the page.

7. Change the color of the square to light blue; you will need to ungroup the objects.

8. Change the colors of the rectangles. Make one medium blue and the other red.

9. Add a shadow to each of the rectangles.

10. Regroup the objects.

11. Save your work as ART085.

Continued on the next page

12. Open a new document and insert of frame in the upper left hand corner. The edge of the frame should be even with the margins of the page. The frame needs to be approximately 2¼" by 2¼" square.

13. Key the letter shown below. Position your return address to the right of the frame. Increase the point size of the text. Choose a size that keeps the address on one line.

14. Save your work as ACT085.

15. Copy the art from ART085 and paste it in the frame. Adjust the text so the return address is even with the red box.

16. Save your work.

17. Print one copy. Use a color printer if available.

18. Close the document.

Name • 123 Main Street • Hometown, ST 00000

Current Date

Michael R. Nickson, Registrar
Lakeview Community College
3324 Clearlake Ave
Lakeland, MN 55927

Dear Mr. Nickson:

Please send an official copy of my transcript to me at the address shown above. My student identification number is 97-9888-144.

A check for $5.00 is enclosed for the processing fee.

Sincerely,

Student's name

Enclosure

ACTIVITY 86

Drawing and Inserting Art

OBJECTIVES

Estimated Time: 20 minutes

+ Create a drawing
+ Insert a drawing in a spreadsheet

You asked a random group of customers which flavor of ice cream they prefer. You are showing your results on a spreadsheet.

INSTRUCTIONS

1. Create a new spreadsheet.

2. Key the data shown below.

3. Save the spreadsheet as ACT086.

4. Draw an ice cream cone and insert it in column C next to the data.

5. Save your work and print the spreadsheet.

6. Close the spreadsheet.

	A	B	C
1	Ice Cream Survey		
2			
3	Flavor	Number	
4	Vanilla	38	
5	Chocolate	22	
6	Strawberry	15	
7	Peppermint	10	
8	Rocky Road	5	

ACTIVITY 87   Drawing and Inserting Art

OBJECTIVES   **Estimated Time: 20 minutes**

• Create a drawing
• Insert a drawing in a database form

You are an intern in the office of a large retirement community. For increased safety and security, parking permits are being issued to all residents with motor vehicles. You are creating a database for keeping track of the permits and the residents cars. To add interest to the database form, you decide to add some art.

INSTRUCTIONS

1. Create a new database; name it ACT087.

2. Create a data entry form similar to the one shown on the next page. Use clip art for the automobile and draw the parking permit.

3. Save your work.

4. Enter the data shown below for the first record.

5. View the next record. The fields will be blank, but the art will appear on the form.

6. Print the first record as a form.

7. Close the database.

Clifton R. Macke
Cottage 363
555-5861
1995 Ford Taurus
Arizona License JVB 871
Permit Number 049, issued 3/27/95

Last Name: _____   Cottage Number: _____

First Name: _____   Home Telephone: _____

Middle Name/Int: _____

Car Make: _____

Car Model: _____

Car Year: _____

Car License: _____

State: _____

```
┌──────────────────────────────┐
│        Parking  Lot  A        │
│       Permit  Number          │
│             000               │
│      Beechridge  Village      │
└──────────────────────────────┘
```

Permit Number: _____

Date Issued: _____

ACTIVITY 88   Copying Text to Spreadsheet

OBJECTIVES   **Estimated Time: 20 minutes**

• Copy text from a document to a spreadsheet

You show a friend the list of NBA coaching statistics you are keeping. She suggests you calculate the percentage of wins.

INSTRUCTIONS

1. Create a new document.

2. Key the text shown below using tabs.

3. Save your work as ACT088.

4. Highlight the text and copy it.

5. Open a new spreadsheet and paste the text you copied from the document ACT088.

6. Save the new spreadsheet as ACT088. (The extension of the word processing and spreadsheet files will be different.)

7. Adjust the column widths of the spreadsheet.

8. Calculate the percentage of wins in column D.

9. Save your work and print the spreadsheet.

10. Close the spreadsheet and the document.

Most All-Time Coaching Victories
(Through the 1994 Season)

Coach	Wins	Losses
Red Auerbach	938	479
Lenny Wilkens	926	774
Jack Ramsy	864	783
Dick Motta	856	863
Bill Fitch	845	877
Cotton Fitzsimmons	805	745
Don Nelson	803	573
Gene Shue	784	861
John MacLeod	707	657
Pat Riley	701	272
Red Holzman	696	604

ACTIVITY 89 Copying Text to Database

OBJECTIVES Estimated Time: 20 minutes

• Copy text from a document to a database

You are keeping a list of local merchants who have advertised in the program for your drama group productions. The current list fits nicely on a single sheet of paper, but you expect the list to grow. You decide to convert the list from a text document to a database.

INSTRUCTIONS

1. Create a new document.
2. Key the text shown below using tabs.
3. Save your work as ACT089.
4. Highlight the text and copy it.
5. Open a new database and paste the text you copied from the document ACT089. Paste the data in list view.
6. Save the new database as ACT089. (The extension of the word processing and database files will be different.)
7. Switch to form view and rename the fields. Use appropriate field names such as Business, Contact, Telephone, and Ad Size.
8. Adjust the field width.
9. Save your work and print the database form for The Bean Counter.
10. Close the database and the document.

Beacon Deli and Meats	Harold Beacon	555-7756	quarter page
Sabrina's Hair Designs	Sabrina LaSalle	555-2111	full page
The Cookie Jar	J. B. Groh	555-4433	half page
Creative Solutions	Terry Tayloe	555-3644	quarter page
Frametastic	Lyle Clark	555-5254	half page
Amanda Wnek, DMD	Katherine Glasier	555-1990	quarter page
The Gallery on Main	Anna Ghizawi	555-2787	full page
Vista Travel Network	Nidal McCarty	555-9300	quarter page
The Bean Counter	Connie Dektas	555-6060	half page
Citizens Bank	David Brumenschenkel	555-8777	half page
Rindarlie Dance Studio	Vivian Rindarlie	555-6004	full page

ACTIVITY 90

Copying Data to Document

OBJECTIVES

Estimated Time: 20 minutes

• Copy spreadsheet data to a document

You are doing a report of the ecosystems of the world's largest desserts. To highlight the text of your report, you want to insert data from the spreadsheet you have developed.

INSTRUCTIONS

1. Key the text shown below.

2. Save your work as ACT090. Do not close the document.

3. Open the spreadsheet file you created in Activity 47, ACT047. If you have not yet completed Activity 47, do so now.

4. Highlight the data in the spreadsheet in ACT047 and copy it. Include the column headings.

5. Switch to the document ACT090 and paste the data you copied from the spreadsheet in between the two paragraphs of text. The data will appear in the word processing document as a table.

6. Edit the column widths of the table if necessary.

7. Center the table.

8. Place a border around the table and add gridlines.

9. Save your work and print the document.

10. Close the document and the spreadsheet.

The ecosystems of the world's deserts are among the most fascinating on earth. Even without irrigation, plant an animal life exist in deserts. The scope of this paper is limited to the six largest deserts in the world. The table below identifies these the deserts by name, location, and size.

Notice that the largest desert, the Sahara, is seven times as large as the second largest desert, the Gobi. The other four deserts are very similar in size. The difference in size among the Great Victoria, Gibson, Rub'al-Khali, and Kalahari is only 25,000 square miles.

ACTIVITY 91 Copying Data to Database

OBJECTIVES **Estimated Time: 30 minutes**

- Copy spreadsheet data to a database

You are keeping track of the World Figure Skating Champions using a spreadsheet. After keying some of the data in a spreadsheet, you decide that a database might be more suited to your needs.

INSTRUCTIONS

1. Key the data shown on the next page. Use copy and fill features to save time.

2. Save your work as ACT091.

3. Highlight the data in the spreadsheet and copy it. Do not include the column headings.

4. Open a new database. Switch to list view.

5. Paste the data you copied from the spreadsheet.

6. Save your work as ACT091. (The extension for the database file will be different than the spreadsheet file.)

7. Switch to form view and name the fields appropriately. You should have a record for each year.

8. Edit the field widths to accommodate the content.

9. Add a field for Ice Dancing. You will need it starting with the 1952 World Championships.

10. Save your work and print the records for 1901 and 1909.

11. Close the database and the spreadsheet.

Year	Location	Men's name:	Men's country:	Ladies' name:	Ladies' country:	Pairs names	Pairs country
1896	St. Petersburg	Gilbert Fuchs	Germany				
1897	Stockholm	Gustav Hugel	Austria				
1898	London	Henning Grenander	Sweden				
1899	Davos	Gustav Hugel	Austria				
1900	Davos	Gustav Hugel	Austria				
1901	Stockholm	Ulrich Salchow	Sweden				
1902	London	Ulrich Salchow	Sweden				
1903	St. Petersburg	Ulrich Salchow	Sweden				
1904	Berlin	Ulrich Salchow	Sweden				
1905	Stockholm	Ulrich Salchow	Sweden				
1906	Munich	Gilbert Fuchs	Germany	Madge Syers	Great Britain		
1907	Vienna	Ulrich Salchow	Sweden	Madge Syers	Great Britain		
1908	Troppau	Ulrich Salchow	Sweden	Lily Kronberger	Hungary	Hubler & Burger	Germany
1909	Stockholm	Ulrich Salchow	Sweden	Lily Kronberger	Hungary	Johnson & Johnson	Great Britain
1910	Davos	Ulrich Salchow	Sweden	Lily Kronberger	Hungary	Hubler & Burger	Germany
1911	Berlin	Ulrich Salchow	Sweden	Lily Kronberger	Hungary	Eilers & Jakobsson	Germany & Finland
1912	Manchester	Fritz Kachler	Austria	Opika von Meray Horvath	Hungary	Johnson & Johnson	Great Britain

ACTIVITY 92
Linking and Embedding

OBJECTIVES

Estimated Time: 30 minutes

* Link a spreadsheet to a document
* Embed a spreadsheet in a document

As a customer service representative you file a weekly report on your activities. You report on all of your activities for the week including the number of calls you answered each day.

INSTRUCTIONS

1. Create a new spreadsheet and key the data shown below. Use copy and fill features to save time.

2. Calculate the total number of calls each day and the total for the week.

3. Save your work as ACT092 and close the spreadsheet.

	A	B	C	D	E	F	G	H	I
1					Number of Calls Per Day				
2		Sunday	Monday	Tuesday	Wednesday	Thursday	Friday	Saturday	Total
3	7:00 a.m.			11					
4	8:00 a.m.			18	17	18	18		
5	9:00 a.m.			12	10	9	11	12	
6	10:00 a.m.			14	19	16	17	15	
7	11:00 a.m.			0	15	17	18	12	
8	12:00 p.m.			32	31	28	27		
9	1:00 p.m.			25	0	0			
10	2:00 p.m.			15	20	18			
11	3:00 p.m.			16	16	14			
12	4:00 p.m.			22	27	26			
13	5:00 p.m.				21	18			
14	6:00 p.m.					14			
15	7:00 p.m.								
16	8:00 p.m.								
17	Totals								

Continued on the next page

4. Create a new document and key the text shown below.

5. Save your work as ACT092B. Create a duplicate document by saving it as ACT092A.

6. With ACT092A open, link the spreadsheet named ACT092 to the document.

7. Save your work and close ACT092A.

8. Open ACT092B if it is not already open.

9. Embed the spreadsheet named ACT092 in the document.

10. Save your work and close ACT092B.

11. Switch to the file manager and compare the file size of ACT092A with that of ACT092B. ACT092B should be larger because the spreadsheet is embedded in the file.

Weekly Report   **Week Ended Saturday, July 9**
Student's Name

Backorders
The ship date for #97-123A is listed as July 1, but there is no stock. What should we be telling customers?

Customer Complaints
Item #97-465B looks black on page 28 of the Winter Catalog, but it is not available in black.
Item #97-999J is running small. Should we suggest a size larger?

Equipment
The new headsets are great. Besides being comfortable, the sound quality is excellent. Thanks.

Telephone Log

---

12. Return to the word processor and open ACT092A. Edit the spreadsheet that is linked to this document. Use the data shown below.

13. Save your work.

14. Open ACT092B and edit the spreadsheet that is embedded in this document. Use the data shown below.

15. Save your work.

16. Print ACT092A and ACT092B.

17. Close all files.

| Thursday | 2:00 p.m. | 13 |
| Friday | 8:00 a.m. | 16 |

ACTIVITY 93

Linking Data

OBJECTIVES

+ Link spreadsheet data to a document
+ Update linked files

You are preparing a memo concerning the 1996 sales figures. You want to add emphasis to the memo by including charts.

INSTRUCTIONS

1. Create a new spreadsheet and key the data shown below.

2. Calculate the total goal and total sales.

3. Save your work as ACT093.

4. Create a chart to show the relationship between quarterly goals and sales.

5. Create a second chart to show the relationship between the yearly goal and total sales for 1996.

6. Save your work.

	A	B	C
1		Goals	Sales
2	Q1	2500	3300
3	Q2	3000	2200
4	Q3	3500	4200
5	Q4	3500	4200
6			
7		Goal	Sales
8	1996		

Continued on the next page

7. Switch to the word processor and create a new document.

8. Key the text shown below.

9. Save your work as ACT093. Do not close the document

10. With the document open, switch to the spreadsheet and copy the quarterly goals and sales section.

11. Paste the spreadsheet data in the document between the two paragraphs. Use Paste Special to link the spreadsheet to the document.

12. Save your work.

13. Switch to the spreadsheet and copy the first chart.

14. Paste the chart in the document after the last paragraph. Use Paste Special to link the spreadsheet to the document.

15. Copy the second chart from the spreadsheet and paste it in the document.

16. Save your work.

17. Print the memo.

18. Switch to the spreadsheet and change the goal for the second quarter to 2000.

19. Switch to the word processor.

20. Check to see if the change you made in the spreadsheet is reflected in the three items that are linked to the memo.

21. Close all files.

Memorandum

To: Sales Team
From: Sales Manager
Date: January 4, 1997
Subject: 1996 Sales Figures

The final sales figures for 1996 confirm that you did an outstanding job last year. Congratulations and thank you for your efforts.

The quarterly breakdown is shown in Chart 1. We were above goal for three quarters last year. While the second quarter was disappointing, Chart 2 shows the overall success of 1996.

ACTIVITY 94   Embedding a Chart

OBJECTIVES   **Estimated Time: 30 minutes**

- Embed a chart in a document
- Update an embedded chart

   You are preparing a flyer about the exercise classes to be held at the community center. While keying the text you decide to add a chart as part of the flyer.

INSTRUCTIONS

1. Create a new document and key the text shown on the next page.

2. Embed a chart in the document.

3. Enter the data shown below to create the chart.

4. Save your work

5. Print the document.

6. Open the chart and change the times allotted to the activities.

7. Compare the updated document to the earlier version that you printed.

8. Save your work and close the document.

	Slice A	Slice B	Slice C	Slice D
	15-Minute Warm Up	20-Minute Aerobics	15-Minute Toning	10-Minute Cool Down
Pie 1	15	20	15	10

Continued on the next page

Community Exercise Program
Winter Workout

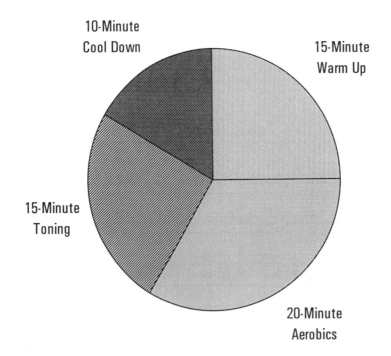

10-Minute Cool Down

15-Minute Warm Up

15-Minute Toning

20-Minute Aerobics

Enroll Today

Call 555-1100 to reserve your spot

Do it for Your Health – Do It for Fun

ACTIVITY 95

Embedding Data

OBJECTIVES

Estimated Time: 30 minutes

• Embed word processing in database form

You are creating the database to be used to track the holiday wish lists at the community center. You decide to embed a word processing document in the form. You will use this document to provide information to volunteers as they enter data.

INSTRUCTIONS

1. Create a new database; name it ACT095.

2. Create a form similar to the one shown on the next page.

3. Embed a word processing document at the bottom of the form.

4. Key the text shown below into the embedded document.

5. Enter data for three records.

6. Save your work.

7. Browse the three records and notice the word processing document appear in every form.

8. Open the word processing document and change the text to italics.

9. Save your work and print the third record.

10. Close the database.

Many individuals and families who participate in the Wish List Program provide more than the three requested items. Use the Comments field to identify special interests, favorite colors, etc.

Requested 10/24/97	Requested 10/24/97	Requested 10/25/97
#410	#410	# 411
Drew	Krystal	Siobhan
Male	Female	Female
Age 4	Age 22	Age 12
Size 4T	Size 12	Size 14
Fire Truck	Alarm Clock	Paint Set
Soccer Ball	Slippers	Books
Coloring Books	Sweater	Hat and Gloves
		Wants to be an artist

Continued on the next page

Wish List

Date of Request: _____   Date Assigned: _____

Family ID#: _____

First Name: _____

Gender: _____   Age: _____   Clothing Size: _____

Item 1: _____

Item 2 : _____

Item 3: _____

Comments: _____

_____

_____

ACTIVITY 96

Creating a Form Letter

OBJECTIVES   **Estimated Time: 30 minutes**

- Create a form letter
- Merge data with form letter
- Print a form letter and matching envelope

You have scheduled employment interviews for several candidates. You decide to create a form letter to confirm the dates and times of these interviews.

INSTRUCTIONS

1. Create a database; name it ACT096.

2. Enter data for each employment candidate. See interview schedule on the next page.

3. Save your work.

4. Switch to the word processor and create a form letter. Use the text shown on the next page and data fields you created in the database.

5. Save the form letter as ACT096. (The extension will be different for the database and word processing files.)

6. Merge the data with the form letter.

7. Print only the letters to candidates who have interviews scheduled on March 28.

8. Print envelopes for the letters you printed.

9. Close the database.

Interview Schedule

Dan McKillip
March 26
1:30 PM Ellen Tabacchi   5612 Clay Ct   Red Wing   MN 55066   Aerobics Instructor
3:30 PM Christina Au   626 Sutton Ave   San Francisco CA 94105   Fitness Coordinator
March 28
3:30 PM Victor Valdes   1855 Borden St   Oakland   CA 94612   Fitness Coordinator
March 30
1:30 PM Jani Sung   101 Webster Dr   San Francisco CA 94103   Aerobics Instructor
3:30 PM Anita Sanders   550 Alpine Rd   San Jose   CA 95128   Fitness Coordinator

Randi Otten
March 28
1:00 PM John Murata   3324 Ridge Ln   Littleton   CO 80123   Skating Instructor
March 29
1:00 PM Danielle Meyer   944 Kendell St   Portola Valley CA 94028   Skating Instructor
March 30
9:00 AM Duncan Carr   120 South Ash   Oakland   CA 94612   Skating Instructor
1:00 PM Marta Place   935 Short Rd   San Mateo   CA 94402   Skating Instructor
3:00 PM Kari Vanagas   1212 Maxwell St   San Carlos   CA 94070   Skating Instructor

Bay Area Sports Club

3600 Bayview Highway   Oakland CA 94612   (510) 555-6300

«First Name» «Last Name»
«Address»
«City» «State» «Zip Code»

Dear **«First Name» «Last Name»**:

Thank you for your interest in the **«Position»** position with The Bay Area Sports Club. You are schduled to meet with **«Interviewer»** on **«Interview Date»** at **«Interview Time»**.

If you need to contact us prior to the interview, please call me at 555-6363.

Sincerely,

Student's Name
Human Resources Specialist

ACTIVITY 97

Generating Labels

Requires ACT096 from Activity 96.

Estimated Time: 15 minutes

OBJECTIVES

• Generate and print labels

In addition to the letter you sent about employment interviews, you now need to send a packet of material to each candidate. You decide to generate labels for the mailing using the database you created for the letters.

INSTRUCTIONS

1. Select labels.

2. Open the database ACT096. If you have not already completed Activity 96, do so now.

3. Create a report to generate mailing labels. Use settings that match the size and format of the labels you have selected.

4. Generate and print the mailing labels in zip code order.

5. Close the database.

ACTIVITY 98

College Application Project, Part 4

OBJECTIVES   **Estimated Time: 45 minutes**

• Use integrated capabilities of software

Applying to colleges is a major project. This is the kind of project where integrated software can simplify the process.

Activity 98 is the final activity devoted to the college application project. In this activity you will use some of the advanced capabilities of your software.

INSTRUCTIONS

1. Review Activities 29, 59, and 79 before you continue with this activity.

2. Develop a story for your school or community newspaper about the college application process.

3. Use a database to help organize your data.

4. Use word processing to key the story.

5. Use spreadsheets to analyze data and create charts and graphs.

6. Add graphics, including charts, clip art, and original art.

7. Save the files you create using the filenames ACT098A, ACT098B, etc.

ACTIVITY 99

Employee Benefits Project, Part 4

OBJECTIVES

Estimated Time: 45 minutes

• Use integrated capabilities of software

You are part of a team working on an employee benefits project. As you work on this project you will use many of the capabilities of an integrated software package.

Activity 99 is the final activity devoted to the employee benefits project. In this activity you will use some of the advanced capabilities of your software.

INSTRUCTIONS

1. Review Activities 30, 60, and 80 before you continue with this activity.

2. Develop a personalized document about the employee benefits. Include information about the benefit programs offered. Also, create a profile of the benefits in which each employee is enrolled.

3. Use a database to help organize your data.

4. Use word processing to key the document.

5. Use spreadsheets to analyze data and create charts and graphs.

6. Add graphics, including charts, clip art, and original art.

7. Save the files you create using the filenames ACT099A, ACT099B, etc.

ACTIVITY 100

Fundraising Project, Part 4

OBJECTIVES

Estimated Time: 45 minutes

• Use integrated capabilities of software

You are part of a team working on an fundraising project. As you work on this project you will use many of the capabilities of an integrated software package.

Activity 100 is the final activity devoted to the fundraising project. In this activity you will use some of the advanced capabilities of your software.

INSTRUCTIONS

1. Review Activities 31, 61, and 81 before you continue with this activity.

2. Develop a status report on the fundraising campaign as of September 1. Include a list of donors, pledges, and gifts as of July 1.

3. Use a database to help organize your data.

4. Use word processing to key the document.

5. Use spreadsheets to analyze data and create charts and graphs.

6. Add graphics, including charts, clip art, and original art.

7. Save the files you create using the filenames ACT100A, ACT100B, etc.

NOTES

NOTES